Strategy and Entrepreneurship in Arab Countries

Also by M.S.S. El Namaki

El Namaki, M.S.S. (ed., 1999) Strategic Issues at the Dawn of a New Millennium, Lansa

Harald Sander, KwaS. Kim, Stephen F. Foster and M.S.S. El Namaki (eds, 1999) Economic and Corporate Restructuring, Lansa

El Namaki, M.S.S., van Dijk, M.P. (eds, 1983) Small Scale Industry Promotion in Developing Countries, RVB

El Namaki, M.S.S. (1979) Problems of Management in a Developing Environment: The Case of Tanzania (State Enterprises between 1967 and 1975), Elsevier North-Holland

Strategy and Entrepreneurship in Arab Countries

M.S.S. El Namaki

palgrave
macmillan

First published in 2008 by
PALGRAVE MACMILLAN
Houndmills, Basingstoke, Hampshire RG21 6XS and
175 Fifth Avenue, New York, N.Y. 10010
Companies and representatives throughout the world.

PALGRAVE MACMILLAN is the global academic imprint of the Palgrave
Macmillan division of St. Martin's Press, LLC and of Palgrave Macmillan Ltd.
Macmillan® is a registered trademark in the United States, United Kingdom
and other countries. Palgrave is a registered trademark in the European
Union and other countries.

ISBN-13: 978–0–230–51564–2 hardback
ISBN-10: 0–230–51564–9 hardback

This book is printed on paper suitable for recycling and made from fully
managed and sustained forest sources. Logging, pulping and manufacturing
processes are expected to conform to the environmental regulations of
the country of origin.

A catalogue record for this book is available from the British Library.

A catalog record for this book is available from the Library of Congress.

10 9 8 7 6 5 4 3 2 1
17 16 15 14 13 12 11 10 09 08

Printed and bound in Great Britain by
CPI Antony Rowe, Chippenham and Eastbourne

Contents

List of Tables

List of Figures

Preface

The following book deals with an issue of direct relevance to present day and future outlook of many Arab countries: their business strategies and their entrepreurial initiative. The book explores both issues in terms of commonly accepted conceptual frameworks and explores the adoption of those frameworks within a selection of countries, corporations, and individuals. The approach is mostly case based. Countries included in the analysis were there because of a demonstrated competency, or near competency, at national business strategic thinking or because of the urgent relevance of the issue to today's and tomorrow's strategies. The selected corporations were there because they have been able to look at things through different eyes and measure things by a strategic measure. Individuals were earmarked because of their demonstration of a measure of entrepreneurial initiative. Not all cases were success cases, though. Less than successful and at times failure cases were also referred to. The book is divided into two parts each dealing with an issue. Both parts start with a "generic" component containing an analysis of the conceptual and operational foundations of the issue at hand. This was done in order to facilitate the process of issue analysis within an Arab context, on the one hand and the provision of a framework for issue analysis, on the other.

Foreword

To say that strategic thinking and entrepreneurial initiative are critical issues in Arab countries is an understatement. Almost all Arab countries without exception are going through a process of deep-rooted change triggered by the turbulent geo-political currents of the area and the powerful forces of globalization. Yet the practice of strategy and the demonstration of entrepreneurial competency leave, in many an Arab country, much to be desired. There are achievements but there are many failures. Evidence is abundant. The width, depth, and contextual framework of strategic thinking and entrepreneurship practice seem, in many instances, to be narrow. Education of the subjects gives, more frequently than not, the impression of incompleteness and cultural rootlessness. Advocation of the competencies sounds, very frequently, hollow and devoid of zeal; especially, all of this against a background of windfall oil revenues and massive FDI flows.

Those are the issues addressed in this book. The book provides a journey through the strategic thinking efforts of several countries and corporations and the entrepreneurial attempts of a number of individuals and families in the region. It exploits the needs, the achievements, and the bottlenecks. It provides evidence of successful practices and symptoms of less than successful ones. The ultimate goal is to draw attention to the need for intervention in an area that is pivotal to Arab economic growth and prosperity.

I should like to recognize, here, the influence of many on the views contained in this book. Four specific personalities head the list: His Highness Sheikh Mohammed bin Rashid Al Maktoum (United Arab Emirates), Dr Mahathir Mohamed (Malaysia), Dr Atif Obeid (Egypt) and Mr Long Yongtu (China). His Highness Sheikh El Maktoum, Vice President of the UAE, Prime Minister of the United Arab Emirates and Ruler of Dubai is an Arab leader who conceived a vision, committed his vision to paper and pursued this vision with dedication and zeal. Dr Mahathir Mohammed, the former Prime Minister of Malaysia, provided courage, leadership, acumen and far sight in the way he responded to the Asian financial crisis of 1997 and the way he has managed his country's spectacular economic growth afterwards. Dr Atif Obeid, former Prime Minister of Egypt had the keen strategic instincts that addressed Egypt's privatization needs and Egypt's free-market adjustments. Vice minister Long Yongtu has been China's chief WTO negotiator and the one who managed the intricate process of China's entry into the WTO a process that required wisdom, prudence, and ultimate strategic judgement. All those are individuals that have, in one way or the other, changed the strategic path of their countries and provided an impulse for strategic re-direction and entrepreneurial initiative of their region.

As to entrepreneurs, I should like to signal three, among several. Space would not allow an inclusion of all those original efforts deserving recognition. The first is Dr Hisham Al Sherif whose pioneering work on Internet in Egypt broke new grounds and offered the country a new horizon. The second is Mr Kombiz Eghdami whose B-to-B *web-based solution for the challenges of global sourcing and trade* will take Arab countries into new directions. And the third is Mr Essam El Shawi, the tireless entrepreneur who is trying, in earnest, to introduce solar energy in Arab countries.

Finally, I should like to express a word of thanks for my wife, Ricky, for her genuine support.

Part I
Strategy and Strategic Thinking

Introduction to Part I

The purpose of this part of the book is to provide, first, an analysis of the generic foundations of strategy, strategic thinking and strategic management followed by an application to Arab countries and Arab companies. The question at the heart of the analysis is the extent to which the concept "lives" within Arab leaders and executives and whether their application is conceptually and operationally sound.

Three chapters will deal with strategy formulation in three Arab countries chosen for the success or failure of their attempts. Those countries include the emirate of Dubai, Libya and Syria. We consider the formulation of company strategy. and follow the strategic behavior of three Arab companies: Emirates Airlines (UAE), SABIC (Saudi Arabia), Misr Spinning and Weaving Company (Egypt). One last chapter was confined to a specific strategy pertinent to the economic strategies of many of the countries we are dealing with in the area, i.e. privatization.

Country analysis, all in all, explores the attempts and the potential; company analysis the strategic behavior and the success or failure of that. The privatization segment throws light on the practice and puts forward a novel approach for formulation of strategy in this area.

1
A Conceptual and Operational Framework for Business Strategy

The strategy wonderland

Roots and history

Strategy and strategic planning are children of the 1960s. Their fathers, Igor Ansoff and George Steiner, stressed the notion that strategy formulation is a top management function and that strategy making is a systems process where inputs lead to measured outputs. Strategy making, according to those early pioneers, was supposed to be a neat and orderly process. Porter and Hax, the following generation of strategy thinkers, introduced the notion of competition and strategic competitive behavior as dynamic forces within the strategy domain. Strategy became, then, the outcome of turbulence, creativity, competency, and the search for uniqueness within an ever-changing business arena. Others, whose writings appeared later, such as Prahalad and Mintzberg, stressed intent, core competency, sustainable competitive advantage, vision, all as underlying drivers of effective strategic behavior.

Early as well as late entrants into the strategy arena did not agree, however, on a single all-inclusive definition of the phenomenon. Definitions varied, and, as we will explain later, many of those definitions need refinement. The word itself is a derivative from the Greek word *strategos*. Ansoff, Mintzberg, Andrews, and Porter all gave it a connotation befitting an individual conceptual framework and interpretation. Ansoff's definition referred to strategy as "... the common thread among firm's activities" (Ansoff, 1965). Mintzberg's definition stated "... strategy is a pattern in a stream of actions over time" (Mintzberg, 1992). Andrews (Andrews, 1971) defines strategy as "... the pattern of major objectives, purposes or goals and essential policies and plans for achieving these goals, stated in such a way as to define what business the company is in or is to be in and the kind of company it is or is to be". And Porter says that strategy is "the creation of a unique and valuable position, involving a different set of activities ... " (Porter, 1996).

Strategic management as a discipline, and regardless of the author, has four main teachings (Goldsmith, 1995). The first is to look to the future. Know what market or industry you are in and where you want to be. Second, pay ongoing attention to external factors whether technological, economic, political, and social – that affect the organization's ability to get where it wants to go. Third, establish and maintain a position among those external factors and internal organization variables – finances, employees, special skills, and so on. Fourth, strategic management is iterative. It is not something that can be done at the front end of an operation and then dropped; it entails feed back and learning. These principles may seem like common sense, but that does not make them easy to follow. Managing strategy is a process and not a single event. It demands action and follow-up. A successful strategist continuously searches for a point of dynamic balance between an organization's strengths and weaknesses and environmental threats and opportunities.

Though widely endorsed and applied across corporations and industries, strategy and strategic management have come under attack. A major work that challenged the premises and the applied dimensions of the concept is that of Minzberg (Minzberg, 1994): *The Rise and Fall of Strategic Planning*. Minzberg based his critique on three "fallacies" of the planning model:

- Predetermination: This is the concern with forecasting the future and/or attempting to adapt or control that predicted future;
- Detachment: The abstraction of planning from operations; a reliance on hard data to the exclusion of soft data;
- Formalization: The notion that strategy making can be institutionalized; that systems can be designed to detect discontinuities, consider all the stakeholders, and provide creativity.

The result, according to Mintzberg, has been a great failure at great cost to American business and other organizations.

It is the author's contention that Minzberg's critique, though factual, ignores many other positive aspects of both strategic planning and strategic management. A prime contribution of the field is the focus on environmental change and the impact of that change on an organization's fortunes. Also the introduction of an element of creativity into the management process as well as the incorporation of an element of concern for the sense of direction an organization should demonstrate.

Conceptual model

Strategic behavior follows a very logical sequence. The starting point is an analysis of the environment, both distant and relevant, and the organization itself. This analysis should highlight maneuvering space that the organization has, the position that it could occupy within that environment, and the goals and objectives that should be set in order to reach that new position, in the longer term. This analysis should also lead to the process of search for a pattern of strategic behavior. Strategic behavior modes, once identified, should lead to a shift in gear towards action, and action should naturally lead to control (Figure 1.1).

What are strategy, strategic planning, strategic management and strategic thinking? As we said earlier, definitions within the entire strategy arena are not always coherent. The author has, therefore, opted to delineate four definition clusters. The first is the concept itself or the term strategy. The second is the time dimension of the concept or what we commonly call "strategic planning." The third is the management process dimension of the concept or what we label as "strategic management." And the fourth, and last, is the mental dimension or what goes into the mind of those who create strategies, i.e. strategic thinking. Those are four inter-related phenomena and their understanding is essential for any discussion of the issue.

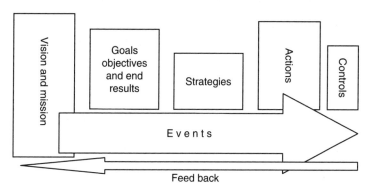

Figure 1.1 A generic conceptual framework for strategy formulation and strategy implementation

What is strategy?

Strategy is the science and art of identifying means for achieving an end.

Strategy is the bridge between goals on the one hand and tactics and actions on the other. Strategy and tactics together straddle the gap between ends and means. In short, strategy is a term that refers to a complex web of thoughts, ideas, insights, experiences, goals, expertise, memories, perceptions, and expectations that provides general guidance for specific actions in pursuit of particular ends. Strategy is at once the course we chart, the journey we imagine and, at the same time, it is the course we steer, the trip we actually make. Even when we are embarking on a voyage of discovery, with no particular destination in mind, the voyage has a purpose, an outcome, an end to be kept in view.

Derived from the Greek, *strategos*, strategy was seen as the "art of the general." Military strategy deals with the planning and conduct of campaigns, the movement and disposition of forces, and the deception of the enemy. The father of modern strategic study, Carl von Clausewitz, defined military strategy as "the employment of battles to gain the end of war." Hence, he gave the preeminence to political aims over military goals, ensuring civilian control of the military. Military strategy was one of a triumvirate of "arts" or "sciences" that govern the conduct of warfare; the others being tactics, the execution of plans and maneuvering of forces in battle, and logistics, the maintenance of an army.

Strategies could have many dimensions. There is a time dimension, a market dimension, a functional dimension, a product dimension, an industry dimension, a gap dimension, a life cycle dimension, etc. We will explore this issue later in this chapter; suffice it to say here, that the use of the term in isolation could mislead and confuse.

What is strategic planning?

Strategic planning is the notion of working within a time framework in order to achieve a stated end.

It is essentially the process of taking inputs (information), organizing and making sense of that information, and producing an output (the plan) that covers a long period of time, and maps out the strategies, goals, and objectives for that period of time. This output, the plan, is expected to keep the organization focused, unified, and likely to succeed in the future, and over a long period of time.

What is strategic management?

In its broadest sense, strategic management is about taking an integrated set of "strategic decisions" touching every managerial aspect of an organization.

It is the process of providing direction, possessing unique competencies, identifying goals, formulating strategies, mobilizing resources, developing actions and exercising control over a foreseeable time frame. It is based on the possession of a core competency and a strategic advantage that would make it possible for the organization to achieve the desired goals.

In other words, strategic management addresses the following questions:

- What business are we in and where do we want to go from here? (Direction, Environmental Scanning);
- What unique competencies do we have and how can we sustain and enhance those? (Sustainable Competitive Advantage or SCA)?
- What goals are driving this business? (Goals);
- What strategies are we following in order to reach our goals (Strategy formulation);
- What resources (skills, assets, finance, relationships, technical competence, and facilities) are required in order to be able to compete? (Resources);
- What actions are we undertaking in order to implement the strategies (Action programming);
- And what controls are we introducing in order to guarantee the congruence of the outcomes with the identified goals and the practiced strategies (Strategic Control).

Strategic management is, in reality, a solid foundation or framework within which all functions of management are bundled together. It is an organization-wide task that starts with scanning of the environment and ends with controlling achievements. It demands the ability to steer the organization as a whole through strategic change under conditions of complexity and uncertainty. It is the highest level of corporate integrative performance.

For strategic management to be successful it should fulfill certain conditions. Prime among those is a shared vision and an action orientation. Secondary but not less important is an element of accountability and control. Last but certainly not least is that it is integrated into the overall management process and supported through a system of participatory involvement.

What is strategic thinking?

Strategic thinking is about visioning and positioning. It is the process of placing a strategically advantaged organization within the right arena. It is a mindset or a way of thinking about a business or an organization. It is vision triggered, innovation- and creativity-based, and system-oriented. It is also the prerogative of top management and falls within its ability to choose a route and set a direction. It is based on the assumption that existing decision making premises are changeable and should be challenged.

Liedkta (1998) takes analysis a step further and suggests the following five attributes of strategic thinking:

- It reflects a systems view that different parts of the organization influence and impinge on one another;
- It focuses on intent – the challenges to existing thinking and assumptions;
- It involves thinking in time. Strategic thinkers understand the interconnectivity of past, present, and future;
- It is hypothesis driven in that it generates ideas and tasks. The creative question "what if" followed by the critical question "If ... then?"
- It is intelligently opportunistic in that it recognizes and takes advantage of emerging opportunities.

Strategic thinking could be looked at from a totally different point of view if one is go back to its roots in war. Strategies are looked at there as what you need when you are conducting one side of a conflict. Since the other side also has a brain, strategies interact in what we may call "a complex, dynamic interaction between two opposing minds."

The object of strategy, again then, is to concentrate a preponderance of power at the decisive point while persuading the enemy to disperse, and thus to employ strength against weakness. This requires a particular way of thinking, a talent for deceit, surprise, maneuver, feints, and often unexpected or indirect approaches to the objective at hand. Napoleon's dispersed marches and concentrated battles made him a champion of the strategic art. (Crocker, 1998)

Strategic thinking could cease to exist if one perceives that there is

(a) no unifying challenge or threat;
(b) no self-evident basis for establishing priorities amongst objectives;
(c) no focus for mobilizing resources;
(d) no discipline for deciding on where and how to deploy them.

Competition and rivalry, then, are considered discretionary matters, and the challenges the organization prepares for are the ones the organization chooses.

Building blocks of the strategy making process

Strategy analysis

Strategy analysis is the process of identifying forces of external influence as well parameters of internal performance. External influences are exerted by an ever-changing environment, with hostile as much as supportive forces. Parameters of internal performance are reflections of an organization's strengths and weaknesses as well as vision, mission, goals, and objectives.

The seven drivers of strategic behavior

Forces of external influence blend with internal patterns of performance in order to produce what we may term drivers of strategic behavior. Those drivers are determinants of the scope, level, volume, and intensity of strategic behavior within an organization. They include:

- Vision and visionary zeal;
- Hyper-competition;
- Sustainable competitive advantage;
- Globalization;
- Organizational complexity;
- Corporate governance;
- Strategic control.

Let us examine those in some detail.

Vision and visionary zeal: A vision is a desired state of the future (El Namaki, 1992). It is neither a dream nor a vague notion of a future either. It is a tangible and reachable state of both environment and organization, a state that is the product of creativity, have a measurable outcome, emanate from a sense of direction, and be able to motivate others and get them to engage. An example is Dupont's vision. It states that it simply want to "... be the world's most dynamic science company, creating sustainable solutions essential to a better, safer, and healthier life for people everywhere."

Sustainable competitive advantage or SCA: An SCA is value creating processes and positions that cannot be duplicated or imitated by other firms, at least not in the medium term. One has to distinguish between distinctive capabilities and reproducible capabilities. Distinctive capabilities are those that can not be replicated by competitors, or can only be replicated with great difficulty. Examples are patents, exclusive licenses, strong brands, effective leadership, teamwork, or tacit knowledge. Reproducible capabilities are those that can be bought or created by your competitors; examples are competencies related to technical, financial, open knowledge, marketing and operations functions.

An SCA could provide the backbone of an organization's strength.

Hyper-competition: Competition has never been as intensive as it is today. There is competition from peers but there is also competition from buyers, sellers, substitutes, and, above all, new entrants (Porter, 1980). The observed increase in intensity of competition could, however, be related to three prime factors: shrinking business cycles, the commoditization of products and services, and the provision of knowledge as a product or service

Organizational complexity: Organizations are getting more complex in terms of structure and management. This is the result of the shift to e-business, corporate integration, virtual organizations, and extended value chains. The strong drive towards merger and acquisition in the United States specifically has contributed, significantly, to this complexity.

Globalization: Globalization connotes movement of goods, services, skills, and capital across borders, organizations, cultures, and economic systems within a capitalist free trade system. The motive for corporations is a reduction in costs (labor, taxes, tariffs, etc.) an improvement in the efficiencies of the supply chain, new market entry, improved operations, and attracting new human resource talents.

Corporate governance: Corporate governance refers to the way the corporation is managed, its relationship with the shareholders as well as with the community. It usually explores the composition and performance of the board of directors; who are they and how good are they? The CEO's role, performance and ethics; the non- executive director's role and compensation. Whether there is an Audit committee and if so how well it performs, director's remuneration level, variation, benchmark and relationship to performance, company relationship with the community and assumption of a degree of social responsibility.

Strategic control: Strategic control means different things to different people. This author suggests a definition that connotes dynamic compatibility between the organization and the environment, over the foreseeable time horizon. This definition could lead to the concept of fitness. The prime building blocks of the organization should fit the environment it is living within. This fitness could relate to the arena where the competitive fight is being conducted, the competencies the organization has or is developing, the resources the organization can muster, and the potential the organization is looking for. There should be a "test" or a measure for each of those elements of fitness.

SWOT analysis

The two dimensions, environment-induced opportunities, and threats as well as organization-rooted strengths and weaknesses, are integrated into what is referred to as SWOT analysis. SWOT is an abbreviation for Strengths, Weaknesses, Opportunities and Threats.

SWOT analysis is an important tool for auditing the overall strategic position of a business and its environment.

Strengths and weaknesses are internal factors. Strength could be a competency in physical distribution or specialist marketing expertise. A weakness could be the lack of a new product or reliance on only a few clients.

Opportunities and threats are external factors. For example, an opportunity could be a developing distribution channel such as the Internet, changing consumer lifestyles that potentially increase demand for a company's products, or the absorption capacity of an emerging market such as China. A threat could be a new competitor in an important existing market, or a technological change that makes existing products potentially obsolete.

SWOT analysis can be very subjective. Company beliefs, norms, and values could have significant impact on considering specific variables as strengths or weaknesses. Position within the managerial hierarchy has an impact too.

The following is an illustration of what could be constituted as strengths or weaknesses for a business organization:

Strengths

- R and D;
- Management team;
- Major client groups;
- Product that can evolve into a product system;
- Leadership qualities of top management;
- Links to centers of excellence.

Weaknesses

- High leverage;
- Low cash resources;
- Narrow composition of the board;
- Weak marketing performance;
- Urgent need for technological shift.

Opportunities

- An emerging market;
- Distribution channels seeking new products;
- Scope to diversify into related markets;
- A newly developed core competency;
- Unique market position.

Threats

- Supplier integrating forward;
- Buyers integrating forward;
- Economic slow down;
- Change in price elasticity;
- Change in cost economies;
- Change in industry scale;
- New entrants.

Drawing conclusions from a SWOT analysis requires prudence and insight. A firm may not necessarily pursue the more lucrative opportunities; rather it may have a better chance at developing competitive advantage by identifying a fit between strengths and upcoming opportunities. An organization may also prefer to overcome a weakness before proceeding with an opportunity exploration. The following matrix provides a projection of the positions an organization may find itself in as a result of one or more of the SWOT elements (Figure 1.2).

Choice of goals and end results

The prime goal of a firm is to achieve an acceptable rate of return on investment or ROI. The viability of a ROI depends on several variables including the cost of capital, the return to risk, and the opportunity cost of the investment.

One can distinguish between growth objectives or goals and efficient objectives or goals. Growth objectives aim at increasing the level of growth variables as sales, assets, market shares, etc. One can segment

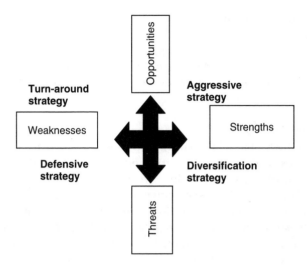

Figure 1.2 The SWOT analysis

those into finance-related growth objectives and market-related growth objectives. Efficiency objectives aim at improving the productivity of the different assets put to use in the course of the business function. Those could include inventories, cash, equipment, buildings; know how, human resources, etc. And one can segment those as Asset-related, Human Resource-related, and Technology-related.

Growth objectives

Finance-related growth objectives

Financial growth objectives focus on achieving acceptable profitability in a company's pursuit of its mission/vision, long-term health, and ultimate survival. Financial growth objectives signal commitment to such outcomes as good cash flow, creditworthiness, earnings growth, an acceptable return on investment, dividend growth, and stock price appreciation (Thomas Strickland, 1998).

The following are examples of financial objectives:

- Growth in revenues;
- Growth in earnings;

- Wider profit margins;
- Bigger cash flows;
- Higher returns on invested capital;
- Attractive economic value added (EVA) performance;
- Attractive and sustainable increases in market value added (MVA);
- A more diversified revenue base.

Market growth objectives

Market growth objectives focus on a company's intent to sustain and improve its competitive strength and long-term market position through creating customer value. They focus on winning additional market share, overtaking key competitors on product quality or customer service or product innovation, achieving lower overall costs than rivals, boosting the company's reputation with customers, winning a stronger foothold in international markets, exercising technological leadership, gaining a sustainable competitive advantage, and capturing attractive growth opportunities (Thomas Strickland, 1990).

Market growth objectives need to be competitor-focused and strengthen the company's long-term competitive position. A company exhibits strategic intent when it pursues ambitious strategic objectives and concentrates its competitive actions and energies on achieving that objective. The strategic intent of a small company may be to dominate a market niche. The strategic intent of an up-and-coming company may be to overtake the market leaders. The strategic intent of a technologically innovative company may be to create a new product. Small companies determined to achieve ambitious strategic objectives exceeding their present reach and resources, often prove to be a more formidable competitor than larger, cash-rich companies with modest strategic intents (Thomas Strickland, 1990).

The following are examples of market growth objectives:

- A bigger market share;
- Quicker design-to-market than rivals;
- Higher product quality than rivals;
- Lower costs relative to key competitors;
- Broader or more attractive product line than rivals;
- A stronger reputation with customers than rivals;
- Superior customer service;
- Recognition as a leader in technology and/or product innovation;
- Wider geographic coverage than rivals;
- Higher levels of customer satisfaction than rivals.

Efficiency objectives

Productivity objectives

Productivity objective are objectives focusing on the improvement of the overall output per man hour levels of the firm. They relate to the productivity of specific inputs as working capital, including inventories, as well as other forms of current assets. The productivity element here refers, mostly, to the speed of the turnover of asset and the improvement of the specific rate of return related to that asset at every turn of the turnover cycle.

Learning objectives

Learning objectives relate to the process of learning that the firm goes through and the impact of that process on productivity and output. Learning could lead to an overall reduction in costs as well as an enhancement of productivity. This is usually reachable through labor efficiency, standardization, and specialization, and methods improvements, technology-enhancement. Better use of equipment, changes in the resource mix, product redesign, value chain effects, network-building, shared experience effects. The learning objectives themselves identify the overall improvement in output as an end result and relate that to one or more of the above mentioned learning triggers.

Return on investment (ROI)

Return on investment is the ultimate goal of the corporation and the goal that should explain the risk element involved in the business venture. Return on investment is the outcome of both growth and efficiency goals outlined above. Measuring a return on an investment requires dividing returns from that investment by the inputs into that investment; the result is expressed as a percentage or a ratio. It is a very popular metric because of its versatility and simplicity at all life cycle stages of a firm or a corporation. It could also lead to important strategic consequences. If an investment does not have a positive ROI, or if there are other opportunities with a higher ROI, then the investment should be reconsidered. This reconsideration is a strategic choice.

The method of calculation of a return on investment can be modified to suit the situation and a lot depends on what one includes in what is considered a return and what is considered an investment. The term in the broadest sense just attempts to measure the profitability of an investment.

Final note

Let us stress, at the end of this part, that strategic behavior connotes resort to a wide range of concepts and that one should delineate the one concept from the other.

• Vision is the prime guiding spirit of the organization;
• Mission statement is an expression of the reason d'être or the reason of existence of the corporation;
• Goals and objectives are desired end results;
• Strategies are media for goal reach;
• Actions are translations of strategies into programs and activities.

Strategic choice or strategy formulation

This process of expressing a strategic choice or formulating a strategy involves understanding the nature of stakeholder expectations, market and competitive conditions and an organization's vision and goals. Strategy choice or strategy formulation could involve either of four approaches or a combination of two or more. The first approach is the mental one: we think and we develop a state of mind. The second is proactive where we express wishes or intent (Hamel 1994). The third involves analysis; we analyze issues and depend on the analytical outcome. And last but not least, we take temporary decisions and let those evolve, over time, into a strategic pattern. Whether to go for thinking, analysis or any of the other alternatives depends on a number of factors. These include the position the organization is in, the resources the organization possesses (financial, human and competencies), current strategy, degree of external dependence, risk tolerance, internal disputes, timing, and anticipated competitive reaction.

Analysis is the most observed pattern. Analysis has its roots in two models that were developed in the early stages of strategy evolution. The first is Ansoff's growth matrix and the second is BCG's portfolio. Ansoff's growth matrix traces two decision variables, product and market, over time and could be regarded as a time-based tool. BCG's portfolio analysis embodies the dynamics of capitalist or free market thinking and the way business is viewed as a series of transactions aiming at return maximization. The SBU is a medium of transaction and SBU possession or dispossession is a function of factors that rise above a preference for a product or an industry or a passion for a technology.

Ansoff's growth matrix

Ansoff's product/market growth matrix (Figure 1.3) suggests that a business' attempts to grow depend on whether it markets new or existing products in new or existing markets. New products and markets could relate to the existing products and markets or could be distant and unrelated.

The output from the Ansoff product/market matrix is a series of suggested growth strategies that set the direction for the business strategy. These are described below:

Market penetration: Market penetration is a growth strategy where the business focuses on selling existing products into existing markets. Market penetration seeks to achieve four main objectives:

1. Maintain or increase the market share of current products,
2. Secure dominance of growth markets.
3. Restructure a mature market by driving out competitors.
4. Increase usage by existing customers.

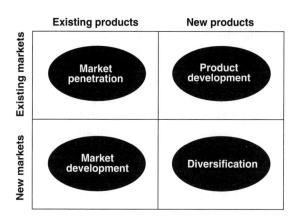

Figure 1.3 Ansoff's growth matrix

Market development: Market development is a growth strategy where the business seeks to sell its existing products into new markets. There are many possible ways of approaching this strategy, including entry into new geographical markets; new product dimensions or packaging, new distribution channels, different pricing policies to attract different customers or create new market segments

Product development: Product development implies the introduction of new products into existing markets. This strategy may require the development of new competencies and requires the business to develop modified products which can appeal to existing markets.

Diversification: Diversification is a growth strategy where a business markets new products in new markets. This is an inherently more risk strategy because the business is moving into markets in which it has little or no experience.

BCG portfolio analysis

The BCG matrix is a strategy formulation tool that creates a close association between a strategy and two prime variables: the relative market share and the rate of industry growth. The purpose of the analysis is to determine the best strategy for each attribute or combination of attributes. The result is the identification of four areas of those combined attributes: the High Growth Rate, High Market Share area or Star, the Low Growth Rate, High Market Share area or Cash Cow, the Low Growth Rate, Low Market Share or Dog, and the High Growth Rate, Low Market Share area or question mark.

Stars are usually the promising SBUs and the relevant ones for the longer term. Their high growth rate requires heavy investment, but it is highly likely that they will reward the attention by producing high margins and strong cash flow. Cash cows should attract attention only to the extent that investment there should protect market share and cash flows. Because of their maturity, cash cows typically do not require much development capital anyway. Cash cows are an extremely valuable asset to the business. Without them, the firm would need to rely far more heavily on external capital for funding the growth of stars, or troubleshooting question marks. Innovation in cash cows is typically aimed at increasing cash flow, for instance by reducing transactional costs so as to increase margins.

Dogs are symbols of poor growth. Strategic behavior there is most likely to be of the divestment and or end gap type. This implies withholding further investment, milk for any cash that can be generated and then divest, selling the business to another firm or closing it down, or if a part of the business is promising enough, focusing on growing that niche practice only.

Question marks have uncompetitive cost structures because of low market share, and could develop one of two ways. If market share can be grown, then they may become stars and later, cash cows. If not, then as maturity sets in, growth slows as price competition heats up and they turn to dogs. Careful analysis is required to determine whether to invest in growing market share. The BCG model suggests that if a question mark has worthwhile prospects, investment should be made to grow market share (Figure 1.4). If not, then that brutal reality needs to be faced and no further investment made.

As we said earlier, the BCG is a dynamic strategy formulation tool that lends itself to broad application.

Strategy implementation

Often the hardest part. When a strategy has been analyzed and selected, the task is then to translate it into organizational action. The following chart provides a view of the outcome of strategy implementation under different conditions of execution. A combination of sound strategy and sound execution provides a high probability of successful reach of the identified objectives. A flawed strategy combined with a flawed execution could result into a doom scenario. Marrying a sound strategy to a flawed execution could only lead to murky performance and the opposite could spell disaster!

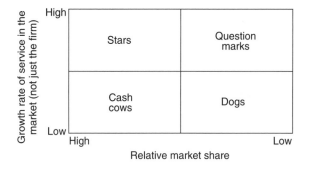

Figure 1.4 The BCG portfolio matrix

Strategic change is implemented through a series of steps that an executive must follow if the change process is to succeed. The first step in the change process is determining the need for change. The second step is identifying the obstacles to change that may prevent a company from reaching its desired future state. Obstacles to change are found at the corporate, divisional, functional, and individual levels. Important obstacles include the inertia produced by an organization's present strategy, structure, culture and differences in divisional and functional goals and interests. The third step is to search of ways and means of overcoming resistance including the use of power to introduce relevant measure including culture change.

Degree of strategic shift

Success or failure at strategy implementation could depend, to a very large extent, on the degrees of strategic change and whether the suggested strategy or strategies represent a major or a minor strategic shift. Major environmental change may dictate a far reaching adjustment in the premises of the business model and a major strategic shift becomes a necessity. The state of the competitive environment may also point into that direction. A major strategic shift connotes the following:

- Major repositioning;
- Unrelated product development;
- Unrelated market development;
- Technology shift;
- Major portfolio adjustment;
- Major cultural shift;
- Major succession (CEO and Board);
- Minor M&A.

Minor strategic shifts could imply:

- Minor repositioning;
- Related product development;
- Related market development;
- Technology adaptation;
- Minor portfolio adjustment;
- Continuation of current top management;
- Major M&A.

Major strategic shifts are more compelling and far reaching in impact than minor ones. Their implications could touch every aspect of structure, manning, performance, and even technology. Major strategic shifts could require change in:

- CEO profile and orientation;
- Some top and middle management executives;
- Organization Culture;
- Organization structure;
- Resources, financial, human-related, or technology-based.

Top management succession and corporate culture adjustment are probably the most serious implications of a major strategy shift.

Possible CEO and top management succession

Change in CEOs is usually the most dramatic implication of a major strategy shift. The rule is that a CEO should both fulfill the fundamental requirements of a CEO, and match the strategic requirements of the new strategic outlook. As to the basic requirements, a CEO should certainly during a phase of strategic shift, be able to take unpleasant decisions and demonstrate exceptional communication skills. He should also know how to manage power, be able to demonstrate situational leadership, and also be able to manage cultural change. As to his "strategy fit", all depends on the industry, the competitive environment within that industry, the core competencies of the corporation itself, and its strengths and weaknesses.

Strategy-based CEO succession is a treacherous process. Some key questions have to be answered before a fitting CEO may be identified. These may include:

- Has the candidate performed activities and set and achieved goals comparable to those outlined in the firm's strategy map?
- What kinds of results has the candidate had?
- Will the candidate's skills transfer well to the new firm?
- Did the candidate engage and inspire other managers by participating in the implementation of key activities and initiatives?
- Did she/he set and achieve realistic goals, overcoming hurdles along the way?
- What are the potential risks that the candidate will not achieve success in the new firm, even though successful at the former one?

Role of organization culture

Organizational culture or corporate culture is the set of values, attitudes, experiences, and beliefs an organization adopts. Put differently, an organization's culture is the set of norms that create powerful precedents for acceptable behavior within the firm. These unwritten "rules of the road" create expectations around acceptable risk, change orientation, creativity, and innovation, group versus individual effort, customer orientation, extra effort, and more. Culture is a powerful force and can provide an engine to achieve market success or an anchor pulling the firm toward failure.

One of the several methods of examining organization culture and identifying its element's is Charles Handy's. Handy (1985) popularized a method of looking at culture which some scholars have used to link organizational structure to organizational culture.

He classified corporate culture as either:

- Power culture which concentrates power among a few. Control radiates from the center with few rules and little bureaucracy.
- Role culture in which people have clearly delegated authorities within a highly defined structure.
- Task culture where teams are formed to solve particular problems. Power derives from expertise as long as a team requires it. Such cultures often feature the multiple reporting lines of a matrix structure.
- A person culture exists where all individuals believe themselves superior to the organization. Survival can become difficult for such organizations, since the concept of an organization suggests that a group of like-minded individuals pursue the organizational goals.

Corporate culture's of whatever kind could be strong or weak. A strong culture is clear and explicit, allows time for communication, contains a value statement or statements, has everybody sharing values and norms, and implies careful screening of newcomers and encouragement of new culture bearers. This type of culture is of paramount importance to strategy implementation; it could contribute to success or failure of strategy through the provision of a strong support set of norms and values, the provision of system information, motivation of people, creation of a company identity and, finally, creating peer pressure.

It may interesting here to refer to the fact that a lack of culture fit may require a change and this is not a simple feat. Change requires time and a strategy of its own. It generally resorts to three methods: crisis, succession, and rewards. A crisis situation may allow a restructuring of operations and the assignment of new roles and responsibilities. Succession could provide a swift method for replacing old culture endorsers with new culture believers. Rewards may encourage peer desire for equity and recognition. The problem, however, is that those methods are time consuming. A period of three to seven years may be required in an average organization depending on the state of the culture; organizations could die before reaching the desired culture change. Finally, culture change to accommodate strategy shifts may prove to be fatal to the organization itself!

Corporate culture change is a controversial issue and should be approached with great care.

Action programming

Action programming is the medium for strategy conversion into decisions and activities. Action programs are logical sequences of actions that must be undertaken to implement endorsed strategies. They include a step-by-step listing of:

- The goals;
- The strategies to be pursued in order to fulfill the goals;
- Actions to be taken to make the strategies realities;
- Resources to be allocated to the actions;
- People responsible for action taking;
- Operational and managerial control measures for action taking and goal fulfillment.

Control

Strategic control

Strategy analysis formulation and implementation is a waste if there is no strategic control (El Namaki, 2006). Massive energies put into environmental scanning, SWOT, the search for strategic moves, and the management of change is all wasted if there is no strategic control. Yet this is exactly what many companies do today. They confine considerable resources to "where we plan to be" instead of "where we ought to be".

The problem, however, is that strategic control means different things to different people. Definitions, and at times understandings, given by key authors from Anthony to Kaplan, endorse this conclusion. Some definitions resort to the popular and others seek safety into the familiar.

Some place the issue within the management control framework (Anthony and Govindarajan, 1998). Others position it within a "balanced score card" framework implying that the balanced score card provides "strategic control systems that measure efficiency, quality, innovation and customer response" (Kaplan and Norton, 1992). Some others make it even simpler by stating that strategic control is "the process by which managers monitor the ongoing activities of an organization and its members and take corrective action to improve performance when needed" (Hill and Jones, 2004). None of these tackles the core issue of dynamic change and organization fitness within a new set of realities.

The balanced score card

The balanced score card is a control tool that, presumably, provides a measure of strategic control. It focuses on two perspectives: an internal perspective and an external perspective. The internal perspective focuses on employee perspective (how do we look to individual employees and to employee groups), a business process perspective (what must we excel at?), innovation and learning perspective (where are our new products and processes coming from?). The external perspectives focus on customers, shareholders, other primary stakeholders, and secondary stakeholders.

Levels of strategy making

Strategy at different levels of a business

Strategies exist at several levels in any organization – ranging from the corporate or the uppermost level of the business (or group of businesses) to the Strategic Business Unit (SBU), or the "strategic molecule" of the organization.

Corporate strategies focus on the overall purpose and scope of the business to meet stakeholder expectations. This is a crucial level since it is heavily influenced by investors in the business and acts to guide strategic decision making throughout the business.

Business Unit Strategies relate to how a business competes successfully in a particular market. It concerns strategic decisions about choice of products, meeting needs of customers, gaining advantage over competitors, exploiting or creating new opportunities.

Functional strategies are concerned with how each part of the business is organized to deliver the corporate and business-unit level strategic direction. Operational strategy therefore focuses on issues of resources, processes, people (see Figure 1.5).

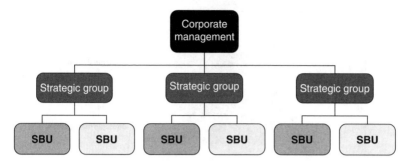

Figure 1.5 Corporate levels of strategy formulation

An SBU is a business unit within the overall corporate identity which is distinguishable from other business because it serves a defined external market where management can perform strategic choices. An SBU could be a division, a product line, or a brand that has an objective and mission different from other company business and that can be marketed independently.

An SBU could also be regarded as a cluster of activities within the organization that represents:

- A financially independent operation, i.e. a business with its own revenues, costs, and results.
- An independent organization with its own building blocks of an organization.
- A clearly delineated market segment.
- A specific technological competency.

The acid test with an SBU or the way to judge whether an SBU is an SBU is simply the ability to divorce or separate this unit from the rest of the organization without adverse repercussions.

Strategy at different levels of the environment

Strategies are formulated at different levels within the environment. There are strategies that are formulated at supranational or global level, there are strategies that are formulated at national levels and there are strategies that are formulated at corporate level. Conventional analysis featuring in a sizable portion of strategy literature focuses on strategy formulation at the corporate level. What an organization, mostly looked at as corporation, does in terms of strategy formulation is the prime

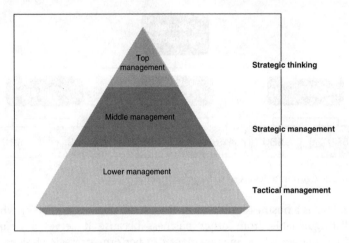

Figure 1.6 The three levels of strategic behavior

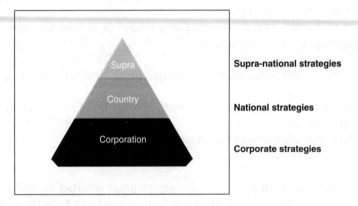

Figure 1.7 "Macro" levels of strategy formulation

concern of the majority of these writings. Strategy formulation at country level or what countries do in terms of strategies is seldom addressed within the main stream strategy literature. What supranational organizations as well as country alliances do in terms of strategy formulation received attention only to the extent that it touched a corporate concern, i.e. within multinational and transnational corporations?

What the author suggests is the existence of three layers or levels of strategy formulation, each with players, system flows, and own environmental forces (Figure 1.7).

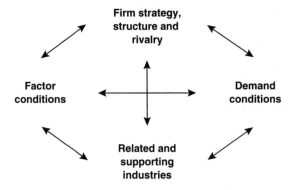

Figure 1.8 Porter's four determinants of national competitive profile

Strategy formulation follows, at all three levels, the basic conceptual framework described above. Work done by Porter in identifying the competitive forces surrounding a nation and how they shape the strategic behavior of that nation is illustrative of this approach. Porter's "Diamond Analysis" (Porter, 1980) rests on an analysis of four forces that combine in order to produce the ultimate competitive positioning of a nation. These are factor conditions, demand conditions, firm strategy and rivalry and, last but not least, related and supporting industries (Figure 1.8).

The fluctuating fortunes of strategy as a discipline

Mintzberg's rise and fall of strategic planning

Strategic planning as conceived by Mintzberg has had heydays and dog days and an analysis of both led him to conclude that the trend was downwards. He put this conclusion in a book, *The rise and falls of strategic planning* (1994) that gained quick fame and considerable response. The book conveys a set of "fundamental fallacies of strategic planning."

Mintzberg came to his conclusion through analysis. First, he established a definition of planning: "A formalized procedure to produce an articulated result, in the form of an integrated system of decision". He further said that formalization means: 1) decomposition; 2) articulation, and 3) rationalizing the process. Second, Mintzberg focused on the planning school that is represented by models developed by Igor Ansoff and George Steiner. There is a review of the increasingly formal, detailed steps, checklists, and techniques of the planning school. Mintzberg argues that under this school's model, strategy formulation is lost, creativity is squeezed out while implementation is greatly elaborated and provides great powers of control.

The result, according to Mintzberg, has been a great failure at great cost to American business and other organizations. The failures are documented with the use of survey results, case histories, and further analysis of the literature. One of the cases discussed is that of General Electric, described by some as having the most effective strategic planning system in existence in the 1970s. This system was dismantled by the one time CEO, Jack Welch.

Mintzberg then argues that the cause of these failures is implicit in the "fallacies" of the planning model, which he describes as the fallacies of:

- Predetermination: This is the concern with forecasting the future and/or attempting to adapt or control that predicted future;
- Detachment: The abstraction of planning from operations; a reliance on hard data to the exclusion of soft data;
- Formalization: The notion that strategy making can be institutionalized; that systems can be designed that can detect discontinuities, consider all the stakeholders and provide creativity.

Each of these fallacies is shown to contribute to the grand fallacy stated earlier.

Mintzberg suggests, as an alternative, that strategy formation should be the province of the decision makers: "In effect, the strategy-making process ... must be seen as an impenetrable 'black box' for planning as well as for planners, around which, rather than inside of which, they work" (p. 331). Thus, says Mintzberg, what is now called strategic planning should be called strategic programming. The key to effectively implementing all the foregoing is to combine analysis and intuition and to recognize planning as the handmaiden of decision making.

Mintzberg's conclusion, regardless of the underlined areas of weakness, has been borne out by the facts of the late 1990s and the early 2000s. The practice of strategy today is more the result of intuitive creativity than rigid system flows. Those early models he has been referring to were, let us remember, the product of a different environment and different market forces. Today's fast environmental change and different market texture make creativity in strategy formulation almost mandatory! And puts strategy formulation within the hands of a different group of individuals from those envisaged in the 1970s and the 1980s, the years Mintzberg is referring to!

Summary and conclusions

Strategy and strategic planning are children of the 1960s. Their fathers, Igor Ansoff and George Steiner, stressed the notion that strategy formulation is a top management function and that strategy making is a systems process where inputs lead to measured outputs. Porter and Hax, the following generation of strategy thinkers, introduced the notion of competition and strategic competitive behavior as dynamic forces within the strategy domain. Others, whose writings appeared later, as Prahalad and Mintzberg, and others, stressed intent, core competency, sustainable competitive advantage, vision, all as underlying drivers of effective strategic behavior.

Strategic management as a discipline, and regardless of the author, has four main teachings (Goldsmith, 1995). The first is to look to the future. Know what market or industry you are in and where you want to be. Second, pay ongoing attention to external factors whether technological, economic, political, and social – that affect the organization's ability to get where it wants to go. Third, establish and keep in touch with those external factors and internal organization variables – finances, employees, special skills, and so on. Fourth, strategic management is iterative.

A few definitions would be in place here:

- Strategy is the science and art of identifying means for achieving an end.
- Strategic planning is the notion of working within a time framework in order to achieve a stated end.
- In its broadest sense, strategic management is about taking an integrated set of "strategic decisions" touching every managerial aspect of an organization.
- Strategic thinking is about visioning and positioning.
- Strategic behavior starts with analysis and ends with control. In between lay the processes of strategy formulation and strategy implementation.

Strategy analysis is the process of identifying forces of external influence as well parameters of internal performance. External influences are exerted by an ever-changing environment, or an environment with hostile as much as supportive forces. Parameters of internal performance are reflections of the organizations strengths and weakness as well as the organization's vision, mission, goals, and objectives.

The seven drivers of strategic behavior are:

1. Vision and visionary zeal;
2. Hyper competition;
3. Sustainable competitive advantage;
4. Globalization;
5. Organizational complexity;
6. Corporate governance;
7. Strategic control.

The two dimensions, environment-induced opportunities and threats as well as organization-rooted strengths and weaknesses, are integrated into what is referred to as SWOT analysis. SWOT is an abbreviation for Strengths, Weaknesses, Opportunities, and Threats.

SWOT analysis is an important tool for auditing the overall strategic position of a business and its environment. Strengths and weaknesses are internal factors. Strength could be a competency. Opportunities and threats are external factors. Drawing conclusions from a SWOT analysis requires prudence and insight.

The prime goal of a firm is to achieve a viable rate of return on investment or ROI. ROI is achieved through growth and efficiency objectives. Growth objectives aim at increasing the level of growth variables as sales, assets, market shares. We can segment those into finance-related growth objectives and market-related growth objectives. Efficiency objectives aim at improving the productivity of the different assets put to use in the course of the business function.

2
Country Strategic Thinking

2.1   Could capitalist strategies work in Syria?

The problem

Capitalist thinking induces the most creative patterns of strategic thinking. And the very shift from non-market systems of economic organization into a market-based structure induces this strategic creativity. Symptoms of strategic behavior are varied, ranging from the introduction of financial market tools and instruments to the increase in private initiative and the restructuring of government functions. This is usually accompanied by a change in the scope and scale of business and the way it conducts its mission.

Syria stands in the middle. Our questions are how much, how soon and how does strategic thinking work there? These and other questions are the focus of this chapter.

The Syrian economy is dominated by agriculture and hydrocarbon extraction. Together they account, in a typical year, for more than 45 percent of GDP. Most production is destined for domestic consumption. Exports are largely confined to oil and cotton. Industry, especially if it is as strategic as oil, is firmly controlled by government through the State enterprise system. Other large industries such as textiles, food processing, chemicals (including pharmaceuticals), and domestic appliances suffer from lack of investment and a critical need for modernization. The Syrian private sector, though fragile, offers much of what the public sector misses.

At the start, we must analyze capitalist and free market thinking in terms of systems theory. It is a managerial analysis. Then we analyze conditions essential for a proper performance of the system in economic, management, and political terms. Finally, we present a critical review of the system framework as well as the probabilities of success or failure of the system in Syria.

Capitalism, capitalist strategies and the free market

Capitalism is an economic system distinguished by private ownership of the means of production. It is also distinguished by market freedom. It is an economic system and not a democratic political system. It is also a system driven by competition, innovation, wealth accumulation, management, and enterprise. It accords paramount significance to the entrepreneur (Schumpeter, 1976) and regards itself as the engine of the progressive process of "creative destruction" capitalism is known for.

Put very simply, capitalist thinking could be viewed, from a managerial point of view, as a system with inputs and outputs, a transformation mechanism, and a feedback loop. It is an open system that exists within an environment and interacts with that environment. General systems theory lends itself perfectly to this kind of analysis. It provides a framework for understanding and integrating knowledge from a wide variety of highly specialized fields (Boulding, 1956). It also allows for system differentiation and system dynamics. There are open systems and closed systems. There are functional systems and cross-functional systems. What matters within the context of this analysis is that general systems theory gives us a powerful tool to examine, analyze and explore the dynamics of capitalism and the inner processes of that ideology.

Inputs in the capitalist system are built around three prime components: premises, players and resources.

Premises of capitalist economic structure include:

- Markets;
- A price mechanism;
- Competition;
- Private ownership;
- Enterprise spirits;
- Free decision making;
- A legal framework;
- A value system.

Players in the capitalist system perform functions essential for the ultimate fulfillment of capitalist ideology. The executive branch, or government, is a player. But so are also the corporations, the entrepreneurs, and the wide variety of functional, sectarian and task-focused institutions operating within the capitalist arena.

As well as inputs, capitalism is a system with outputs and transformation mechanisms. A transformation mechanism is a blend of policies, strategies, and fulfillment efforts exercised in search of value added. Prime among these are:

- Trade policies;
- Industrial policies;
- Monetary policies
- Fiscal policies;
- Wage policies;
- Investment policies;
- Price policies;
- Employment policies.

Also, the following strategies:

- Internally oriented strategies; or strategies where internal growth is the prime lever of economic growth;
- Externally oriented strategies; or strategies where the outward orientation of the economy is the prime medium of growth.

When does capitalism work and when does it fail?

Capitalist thinking is prone to grow and thrive or decline and subside according to the environmental context where it exists. System building blocks will have to be there, complete and sound, for it to exist in the first place. Other enabling conditions could include:

- A sound economic and legal "rules of the game";
- Low enterprise entry barriers and low enterprise exit barriers;
- Continuous policy tuning;
- External orientation of the economy;
- Maximum learning and minimum de-learning;
- A mechanism for coping with income and wealth disparity;
- Optimum market accesses (both own market and external markets);
- Cultural sympathy, a sense of drama, and a will to enterprise;
- Productivity and added value expand the resource base;
- A degree of tolerance to corruption;
- Enterprise spirit.

Problematic performance and tendency to fail could result, on the other hand, from the following factors:

- Extreme income disparities;
- Over-regulation, by government or institutions;
- Unbalanced power play;
- Constrained capital behavior;
- High ethical standards;
- Imperfect competition;
- Low enterprise;
- Restrained price mechanism;.
- Restive labor.

Now the case of Syria

For a capitalist framework to exist in Syria one needs certain conditions. These could be either generic (system specific) or enabling (system enhancing). There also needs to be a process of choice in terms of policy and strategy of the breed of capitalism that the country wants to endorse as well as the set of appropriate values (Tables 2.1 and 2.2).

Table 2.1   System-specific quantitative parameters of Syria 1997–2001

Parameter/Year	1997	2000	2001
Capital base	80	270	205
FDI ($ million)	21	19	21
Gross capital formation % of GDP	–	20.8	20.8
Productivity	29	29	28
Value added in industry as % of GDP	46	49	50
Value added in Services as % of GDP			
Openness of the economy			
Trade in goods as a share in GDP %	55	47	45

Source: World Bank Country Profile, 2002

Table 2.2   Syria's GDP growth 1997–2001

Year/Output	1997	2000	2001
GDP growth (annual %)	1.8	0.6	2.8

Source: World Bank Country Profile, 2002

Are building blocks available in Syria?

The inputs

Capital Market. The basic infrastructure for an active capital market is not in place. A securities market is yet to emerge. The banking sector needs grass roots restructuring. Measures to tune the system to international requirements are yet to be introduced. A bank supervision mechanism is to evolve. Economic policy safeguards to protect both investors and the operations of the securities market are yet to be developed, given a legal framework, and put into practice. A state mechanism for the protection of the private investor especially with regards to investment funds needs to be introduced.

What is being done?

- Investment institutions. A foreign investor's forum is to be established with the objective of improving investment climate.
- Domestic capital resources are fragile given the low per capita GDP and the weak propensities to save and to accumulate capital.
- Foreign capital resources especially foreign direct investment is flowing at a very modest rate. Bias towards oil and gas investment is understandable.
- Entrepreneurship, small business, and private initiative are still emerging. The volume of self-employed is way below the common standard in comparable economies.
- Government institutions are in a stage of transition. Structural change is badly needed.
- Corporate sector, especially State owned enterprises, is in need of massive restructuring with privatization as a major instrument.
- A basic legal framework for private business activities is in the making. A Decree on Licensing, a Law on Freedom of Entrepreneurial Activities and a State Registration of Legal Entities are being talked about. Laws on bankruptcy, banking, and securities and a stock exchange are yet to emerge.
- Although there is a legal provision for property rights, inadequate administration and lack of legal expertise make enforcement uncertain.
- Entrepreneurship, small business, and private initiative are still emerging. The volume of self-employed is way below the common standard in comparable economies.
- Introduction of capitalist values, including private initiative and enterprise, is progressing though the process will take time. It is a cultural change of the type that requires years to gain a full hold.

- Developing a competitive profile is one of the major concerns of the Syrian government. An industrial modernization program is the main vehicle. The program aims at improving the overall policy framework, enhancing the business environment, restructuring industrial institutions, adapting and adjusting critical areas as standards and import and export procedures, competition policy, investment promotion, research and development, consumer protection, industrial licensing, and work safety regulations.

Some very basic premises, resources, and players are there but their quality, volume, and magnitude are still evolving.

Transformation mechanism

Policy and strategy framework

- Investment policies. The general trend is towards creating a climate favorable to foreign investment. New laws are, however, badly needed. Those relate to, among others, anti-monopoly, bankruptcy, pensions, and new accounting procedures and standards.
- Privatization policies. Large-scale privatization through sale of residual stakes in large companies through the stock market is not known yet.
- Fiscal policies. A new tax regime is needed.
- Industrial policies. The government has given preferential treatment to several industries including oil and energy, textiles.
- Wage and labor policies. A new labor law is needed. This should deal with trade union status and workers rights.
- Trade policies. Syria has concluded EU trade agreements and is accommodating that. WTO entry is a remote possibility, under the current conditions.
- Foreign exchange policies. Managed currency floats is happening. Exchange rate stability is the objective.
- Monetary policies. Interest rate plays little if any role in the management of the money supply and operations.

Given this situation, a policy reform is urgently needed.

Economic strategy framework

The government appears to be in the process of opting for a firm strategy. Current moves are towards a degree of external orientation but the road seems to be long before any of the essential measures mentioned below are introduced:

- A gradual removal of tariff and non-tariff barriers to export and import trade;
- Adopting a conducive foreign exchange policy, i.e. a managed currency float;
- Introducing stimulatory measures for exports, especially those of energy and minerals;
- Removing export subsidies and quasi-subsidies.

The output

Output, measured in terms of GDP, is certainly there. The level has wild fluctuations, though.

Feedback

There is a measure of conventional information flow in the system. It is built around formal and informal communication. There are indications that feedback does have an impact and that corrective action is invoked.

Enabling (and disabling) conditions

There are two enabling and two disabling conditions.

1. **Enterprise spirit**. Roots of enterprise lie deep in Syria. Evidence for this subjective judgment can be found in the large population of business migrants, and the rate of growth of self-employment. Whether the entrepreneurial norms such as perseverance, achievement, risk-taking are deeply grounded in the personality traits of the average Syrian is something to be researched more ruggedly in the future.
2. **Learning**. Desire for education and educational achievement is strong in Syria. This is usually a strong force for private initiative and entrepreneurial achievement. Again this needs to be confirmed by research.

Disabling conditions include:

1. **Entry and exit barriers**. Enterprise entry remains, generally, constrained. Administrative procedures constitute the main barrier.

Some of these procedures are prone to malpractice, also. Enterprise exits or bankruptcy is equally difficult. The impression prevails that financial failure does not always lead to bankruptcy.

2. **Tolerance of corruption**. There exists a notion that the capitalist ethic condones a loose base of income flow and a less than optimum approach to division of returns. Also that corruption could, in certain cases and under specific conditions, be an expression of a cultural or societal mechanism for income redistribution.

The chosen breed

A foundation for a capitalist free market system may be emerging in Syria but the question remains which capitalist system? The question is not theoretical but practical and pragmatic. And there is a choice. A no-strings-attached type of capitalism similar to that of the United States or Thailand. Or a tempered variety similar to that of the Netherlands or Singapore. Or it may, finally, pursue a path leading to a Japanese or Korean version. The important point here is that there is a choice and that the choice will have to be made.

What will ultimately determine the choice? Several factors. The first is the vision of the future that is being conceived. The second are economic and political developments in this part of the Middle East. The third is the level of tolerance of the pain associated with the process of transformation. The fourth and last is the speed with which the country wants to move. The fifth are the cultural forces or the values that are buried deep inside Syria's value system. The sixth are domestic political preferences and pressures.

Syria may, in the light of these circumstances express a preference for a quasi-European type of capitalism. This would be a system where:

- The banking system has a dominant role in the process of investment and macro-management of the business sector;
- The securities market plays a secondary role in fund mobilization and management of investments in the economy;
- The government endorses an externally oriented economic strategy linking economic growth to performance within the world market;
- Government stimulates foreign investment and opens the door for foreign direct investment as well as foreign portfolio investment;
- Government follows a balanced budget policy and resists the temptation to use windfall revenues from the energy industry to finance government deficit;

- There is a role for the entrepreneur and the small business sector but not as dominant as that in some other free market economies;
- A welfare system emerges that allows for a broad protection of labor within a structured framework.

A choice of this nature will have far-reaching impact. It will be tantamount to the introduction of new or modified policies for:

- Capital market structure and instruments;
- Economic welfare policies;
- The formula for the division of productivity gains within the economy;
- Scope and scale of private initiative;
- Role of government initiative in economic policy and strategy;
- Pattern of competitive behavior within markets;
- Price and wage policies.

It will be a far-reaching and profound choice.

Summary and conclusions

Free market thinking and capitalist ethics are supreme. Their foothold in Syria is, however, very fragile. This chapter contains an analysis of capitalist thinking along systems theory lines. It projects capitalist doctrine as a system with inputs (premises, resources and players), transformation mechanism (policies, strategies and actions) and outputs (productivity, value added and profits). The system is prone to growth and decline. Factors contributing to growth include an enterprise spirit, a supreme capital market, a free flow of goods and services, and a sympathetic value system. Factors leading to decline include extreme income disparities, unsympathetic attitudes, and lack of enterprise. Basic requirements are enterprise, entrepreneurial spirit, and entrepreneurial initiative.

Syria stands on the threshold of a process of economic transformation. The inputs are still being formulated, the transformation mechanisms are also beginning to operate, and the outputs are a long way down the road.

What is needed is a serious attempt at completing the inputs and giving the transformation mechanism a strong nudge.

Will that happen? That remains to be seen.

2.2   Dubai and Singapore, enroute to a competitive collision?

The problem

Dubai has ambitious economic plans. It is building infrastructure, attracting foreign direct investment (FDI), stimulating MNC entry, enhancing the human resource base, and creating a sound foundation for the service sector. But so also is Singapore, the world' leading competitiveness champion. Singapore is improving productivity, enhancing government effectiveness, integrating technology, attracting multinationals, developing infrastructure, and, finally, innovating (Table 2.3).

Table 2.3   Global Competitiveness Ranking of the first twenty countries according to the World Economic Forum 2004–2005

Country	Global Competitiveness Index		
	2005/rank	2005/score	2004/rank
Finland	1	5.94	1
United States	2	5.81	2
Sweden	3	5.65	3
Denmark	4	5.65	5
Taiwan	5	5.58	4
Singapore	6	5.48	7
Iceland	7	5.48	10
Switzerland	8	5.46	8
Norway	9	5.4	6
Australia	10	5.21	14
Netherlands	11	5.21	12
Japan	12	5.18	9
United Kingdom	13	5.11	11
Canada	14	5.1	15
Germany	15	5.1	13
New Zealand	16	5.09	18
Korea, Rep.	17	5.07	29
United Arab Emirates	18	4.99	16
Qatar	19	4.97	–
Estonia	20	4.95	20

Source: Global Competitiveness Report 2005–2006

Would this put Dubai and Singapore on a competitive collision track?

This is the question that we will try to answer in the course of the next few pages. Analysis will be based on Porters so-called "Diamond Analysis" complemented by the World Economic Forum's framework. Porters' analysis relates to factor and demand conditions, government policy, firm structure, and rivalry. The World Economic Forum's Global Competitiveness Index is wider in scope and goes all the way from the macro economic environment to the institutional framework, and the technological foundation. Both will blend into a 'Diamond'-based, World Economic Forum-enhanced, analysis. Issues will be looked at in terms of the competitive profile of each of the two countries and the likelihood of a collision or collaboration. And whether there is something to learn from all of that.

The research is based on relevant work done on the economic and investment climates of both countries. Results of a few 'Diamond' analyses published earlier as well as the contents of several World Competitiveness Reports were consulted as well. Expert advice was also sought.

The analytical framework

Both Singapore and the United Arab Emirates (UAE), of which Dubai is a member, rank among the top 20 countries in the World Economic Forum's Growth Competitiveness Index analysis. The 2004 issue puts Singapore in seventh place while the UAE is placed in 16th place. The 2005 report put Singapore in sixth place and the United Arab Emirates in 17th. Singapore has consistently outpaced not only the UAE, but is also as recognized a front runner as the Netherlands and the UK (Global Competitiveness Report, 2004–2005).

Would the advanced ranking of both Singapore and the UAE and the striking similarities in their strategies and frameworks inevitably lead to a competitive collision?

Porter's 'Diamond Analysis' (Porter, 1980) (Figure 2.1) and the World Economic Forum's analysis may provide the answer. Porters' approach rests on an analysis of four forces that combine in order to produce the ultimate competitive positioning of a nation. These are factor conditions, demand conditions, firm strategy and rivalry, and related and supporting industries. The World Economic Forum's Global Competitiveness Index looks at the macroeconomic environment, the quality of public institutions and technology and assigns relative weights to each. Both do, to a certain extent, complement each other. Applying these models to Dubai and Singapore produces the following picture:

Country analysis: Dubai

Factor conditions and infrastructure

Infrastructure. Dubai has developed (and continues to develop) a solid physical infrastructure. Road system, power plants, water and sanitation facilities, transportation networks, telecommunication media etc are all developed to a world-class level.

Labor. Dubai population is growing rapidly, driven by economic growth, good quality of life, and a very strong job creation effort. Employment grew by 8.7%, economically active population increased by 4.6 percent, and output per employee expanded by 1.9 percent, between 1999 and 2004.

The Labor Market is, however, strictly regulated. A new labor law allows for the creation of labor unions to ensure labor rights but those will be limited to UAE citizens only. Expatriate workers will be represented through special committees. Composition of the workforce leaves a lot

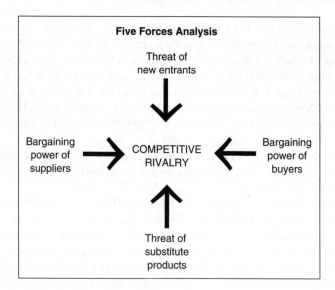

Figure 2.1   Porter's Diamond Analysis

Source: Adapted from M.E. Porter, Competitive Strategy, Free Press, 1980

to be desired in Dubai. There is a quantitative bias towards operators at the expense of R&D-driven knowledge workers.

Capital. Dubai is developing a solid financial infrastructure. Dubai financial market began operations in 2000 and has witnessed an increase in market capitalization; there is a well-developed banking sector, and rapidly developing equity market. The opening of the Dubai international financial Exchange DIFX, will help develop Dubai as a regional and, eventually, global financial hub.

Investment Climate. Investment laws and regulations are federal and are still evolving within the UAE as a whole. At present, the regulatory and legal framework favors local over foreign investors and there are restrictive agency, sponsorship, and distributorship requirements. Companies established in the UAE are required to have a minimum of 51 percent UAE national ownership. There is no income tax in the UAE. There are no consumption taxes either. A single import tariff of 5 percent applies to nearly all imported goods. Incentives are given to foreign investors within the free zones. Sixteen free trade zones operate in the UAE and they serve as major re-export centers to the Gulf region. The waiver of the requirement for majority local ownership is a prime attraction to these free zones.

Government. The Dubai government has been going out of its way in order to create the proper conditions for business. Physical, communication, legal, and institutional infrastructures are actively created. The Government is supporting higher education and research as well. The UAE Government also continues to lead the region in protecting intellectual property rights (IPR).

Demand conditions

Dubai's per capita GDP is comparable to advanced market economies (US$25,770 in 2004) but this can not, solely, propel economic growth. Regional demand is providing, on a *de facto* basis, a broader scope and greater impetus to this economic growth. The central location of the country is making Dubai a 'hub' and a source of products and services for others within the UAE and beyond.

Related and supporting industries

Relatedness is a key factor in the development of industries in Dubai. Clusters are created around the tourism industry, the media industry,

Factor conditions
Capital and infrastructure
are well supplied. Labor is
variable depending on
technology.

Related and supporting
Industries
Strong strategic industry
clusters are evolving.

Firm strategy, structure
rivalry.
Company creation
needs attention. Some
company strategies
need innovation...

Demand conditions.
High GDP per capita allows strong
demand. Regional demand is a boon.

Government
Strategy is clear and bold.
Challenges are being met.
Dynamic outlook.

Figure 2.2   Porter's Dubai Analysis

the information industry, the real estate industry, the finance industry.
and the knowledge industry. Dubai is a trade hub as well.

Firm strategies

Dubai situation is summarized in Figure 2.2.

Singapore

Singapore is moving away from being an efficiency-driven economy to
an innovation-driven economy; this is reflected into the attributes of
the following World Economic Forum's parameters (Tan and Phang,
2005).

Factor conditions and infrastructure

Infrastructure is modern and operationally effective in Singapore. This applies to all sectors including transportation, communication, and energy. Singapore is considered a major physical entry point to South East Asia and performs this function effectively, despite a land constraint.

A Strong Workforce is part of the ecenario of Singapore's growing robust economy. Singapore attracts foreign labour but does not posses sufficient volumes of skilled domestic workers to cope with demands. Singaporean wages are higher than those in neighboring countries.

Foreign Direct Investment and Venture Capital have been attracted by Singapore with considerable success. Financial institutions are comprehensive in coverage and reach.

The Investment Climate is bracing in Singapore. There is a wide range of investment incentives. Foreign and local entities may easily establish, operate, and dispose of their own enterprises. Some businesses, such as banks and insurance companies, need to obtain the relevant licenses before they can start operating.

Several tax incentives are available to encourage foreign companies to make Singapore their regional manufacturing, servicing or financial base. These incentives are also offered to industries which require skilled labor, new and sophisticated technology and equipment.

Tax breaks are also available to a range of businesses. These include the financial services industry, venture capital companies incorporated and operating in Singapore, companies with new capital expenditure of at least S$10 million in new equipment, the export of certain goods, warehousing operations international consultancy services, shipping enterprises, and oil and commodity trading.

MNCs can also apply for incentives under the Regional Headquarters (RHQ) incentive program whereby an MNC operation in Singapore could be an Operational Headquarters (OHQ), a Business Headquarters (BHQ), or a Manufacturing Headquarters (MHQ).

The corporate tax rate in Singapore has been progressively reduced and stands at 26 percent. Capital allowances are available to companies for their industrial buildings, plant, machinery, and the expenditure incurred in acquiring approved know-how or patent rights. Singapore has double taxation agreements with 34 countries.

Singapore's legal system is based on UK law and offers effective means for enforcing property rights. Common law protects and facilitates the acquisition and disposition of all property. Secured interests in property are recognized and enforced.

Singapore has institutionalized and internationalized arbitration through the creation of arbitration bodies and ratification of international conventions.

Government has played a significant role in shaping the economic strategy of the country. A major strength of the Singaporean government is the recognition that the development of ICTs underpinned success in every industry sector. (Harvey *et al.*, 2001). Also the creation of a balanced mix of policies and institutions.

There is a view, however, that there is "too much" government in Singapore. Government "guidance" in the form of financial incentives and approval requirements draws management attention more to the government than the market. Government ownership of assets and enterprises is, also, and despite privatizations, still high.

Demand conditions

Singapore's domestic market, though affluent, can not fully sustain a strong economic growth scenario and there is reliance on the neighboring regional markets.

Related and supporting industries

FDI has contributed and continues to contribute heavily to new manufacturing investment in Singapore. The result is the presence of several multinational corporations and their identification of Singapore as a base for their Asian operations.

Singapore was, however, ranked low in firm-level innovation in 2002, way below most developed economies (World Economic Forum, 2003). Singapore ranks high in technology-using indicators and low in technology-creating indicators.

Singapore ranks poorly in terms of entrepreneurial initiative as well.

Firms, strategy, structure, and rivalry

Singapore situation is summarized in Figure 2.2.

Factor conditions
Capital and infrastructure
are excellent.
Knowledge labor is in
limited supply.

Related and supporting
Industries
Strong strategic
industries with regional
Relatedness. Frequent
industry shifts.

Firm strategy, structure +
rivalry
Firms are world-class
competitors.
MNC are dominant

Demand conditions
Strong. Regional demand traditionally
Supportive

Government
Strategy is dynamic.
Government is alert to
threats.

Figure 2.3   Porter's Singapore analysis

Discussion

The comparative view

The Dubai and Singapore aggregate picture can be projected into the following two tables (Tables 2.4 and 2.5). Both are judgmental reflecting the authors own assessment of the respective issue. And while the first follows Porter's parameters the second borrows some of the parameters utilized by the World Economic Forum.

A careful examination of tables and other material above gives a strong impression that Dubai seems to be following Singapore's learning curve of the 1990s. It is creating a quality infrastructure, involving MNCs, inviting foreign work force, stimulating services, and increasing wages. Many of Dubai's economic policies of today are reminiscent of Singapore's policies of the 1990s. Even Singapore's corrective measures

Table 2.4   Comparative view of Porter's competitive parameters of Dubai and Singapore

Country	Factor conditions	Demand conditions	Firm strategy and structure	Related and supporting industries	Government
Dubai	+	+	+	=	++
Singapore	+	++	++	+	++

Key:
1. Excellent (++);
2. Good (+);
3. Operationally acceptable (=)
4. Poor (−);
5. Critical (−−)

Table 2.5   Comparative assessment of some of the parameters utilized by World Economic Forum for Dubai and Singapore

Prime and derivative parameters	Singapore			UAE		
Macroeconomic environment	+	=	−	+	=	−
1. Investment climate	x			x		
2. Investment incentives	x				x	
3. Employment laws	x					x
4. Disputes	x					x
5. Intellectual property	x				x	
6. Taxation		x		x		
Public institutions						
1. Mix of institutions	x				x	
2. Policy outputs/policies	x				x	
3. Overall quality	x				x	
Technology						
1. R&D investment		x				x
2. Technology implementation	x				x	

of the past few years seem to have a resonance in Dubai's economic thinking. Dubai is trying, for example, to move from a factor driven to a knowledge driven economy. Dubai is also placing services at the core of its economic growth strategy with ambitious goals set for industries such as aviation, telecommunication, tourism, banking, and shipping (services).

Two scenarios could emerge from the above picture. The first is a competitive warfare scenario whereby competition could gradually become tangible in specific sectors, e.g. tourism, aviation, and finance and banking services. This is likely if Singapore loses key industries and feels threatened by an ever expanding Dubai market share in the global market. This could take place in the aviation industry, for example.

The second is a "managed truce" or agreements concluded early enough between the two parties to cooperate and share markets in industries where collision is likely.

What is to be learned?

Dubai could view this issue from two angles: the combative competitive angle and the learning angle.

Learning how to avoid past mistakes

Dubai should learn from Singapore's mistakes and try to avoid some if not all of them. Typical are the wage hikes of the eighties; these have driven out the labor intensive industries but killed, with that, a natural ground for entrepreneurship. The late search for substitute industries was yet another mistake that manifests itself even today. Strong reliance on MNCs has given advantages but resulted into dilemmas when the same multinationals migrated to greener pastures. Lack of a medium skilled workforce is a bottleneck that hampers a proper development of many industries in the country.

Borrowing

Some of Singapore's economic policy principles and institutional framework are worth imitating or borrowing outright. As for policies, those related to investment including the incentives, the legal foundation, and the foreign MNC inflow, are certainly worth closer examination. The institutions, too, include the Economic Development Board and the Board of Investment, examples of a balanced and innovative approach to policy making.

Learn how to prepare for collision

Preparation for a confrontation could cover many arenas. One is the WTO (World Trade Organization), a venue where trade disputes could land. Yet another is developing early strategic alliances with either the multinational corporations operating in Singapore or the Singapore government itself.

Regarding Singapore, the issue may be more complex as it has to develop a growth strategy for decades to come. Dubai is only one of many potential competitors and could be a 'mild' one at that. Stronger competitors will very likely emerge in Singapore's own backyard. Not all of China, but specific Chinese provinces may pose a stronger challenge to Singapore's supremacy in specific industries.

Summary and conclusions

There is reason to believe that a certain degree of congruence exists between the economic strategies of Dubai and Singapore. Dubai is building a massive infrastructure, attracting private investment, stimulating MNC entry, enhancing the human resource base, and building a sound foundation for the service sector. Singapore has been doing the same thing for the past few decades. It is perfecting its infrastructure, enhancing government effectiveness, integrating technology, attracting multinationals, and encouraging innovation.

This congruence could spell good or evil. It could, within an evil scenario, lead to a competitive collision especially in industries such as financial services, aviation, and tourism. It could be benign if it leads to cooperation and strategic synergy.

This chapter explores a country situation along the lines of Porter's Diamond Model. It also resorts to data extracted from the World Competitiveness Report.

Certainly Dubai could learn from Singapore's mistakes and search for pertinent situational strategies.

2.3   The future strategic positioning of Libya in the international market

The problem

Libya is a country of blue skies, massive landmass, and untapped opportunities. The country is blessed with an extensive coast line, stretches of fertile land, favorable weather, industrious population, and ample oil reserves. The country is also sparsely populated and strategically located.

Its small population gives it one of the highest per capita GDPs in Africa. GDP growth has been showing positive trends and is put at 8.5 percent for the year 2005. Libya is also an internationally connected nation with an economy that is integrated into global markets and an Information and telecommunication infrastructure that is quite conducive to the process of economic growth the country is going through.

Libya has maintained a socialist economy where the government is the main player. The government owns major assets, provides employment, sponsors economic initiatives, and supports social programs. The government dominates Libya's socialist-oriented economy through complete control of the country's oil resources, which account for approximately 95 percent of export earnings, 75 percent of government receipts, and 30 percent of the gross domestic product. Oil revenues constitute the principal source of foreign exchange. A shift away from these socialist economies came in the early 2000; initial steps included applying for WTO membership, reducing some subsidies, and announcing plans for privatization and a reduction in government employment. The non-oil manufacturing and construction sectors, which account for more than 20 percent of GDP (2005 data), have expanded from processing mostly agricultural products to include the production of petrochemicals, iron, steel, and aluminum.

Libya's economic growth has been constrained by adverse global political currents, a situation that is changing very rapidly. A question could arise, however, as to the future economic growth strategy and where will the country go from today's favorable position. In this chapter, analysis is based on an analytical strategy formulation model that identifies what one terms Strategic Business Arena's SBAs, or areas of economic and technological strength that a country chooses as the prime vehicle for economic growth. Growth arises, in this case, from a favorable position taken by those SBAs in the international market.

The conceptual framework

Global positioning of Strategic Business Arenas (SBAs)

An observer of patterns of international trade cannot help but hypothesize that some countries appear to view their economic growth strategies in terms of strategic positioning in the international market. This connotes the implicit or explicit definition of an objective strategic position for a set of identified Strategic Business Arenas (SBA), the mobilization of resources in order to attain this strategic position, and a continuous shift among strategic positions and SBAs in order to achieve a country goal. It also connotes the movement of these countries, in the process, down several experience curves and across multiple products, markets, and technologies. Countries like South Korea, Taiwan and, more recently, China have in the course of time adopted what was to them, novel business models and technologies and emerged with a substantial presence in the international market. Those countries appear to have been managing their strategic business arenas as strategic business units within a portfolio, with strategic shifts from areas of low market share and limited relative growth to areas of high market share and high relative market growth (El-Namaki, 1989).

The analysis is based on an adapted version of the BCG Portfolio Analysis. The concept, as we said earlier, was developed in the early seventies and was applied as a tool for identifying the relative position of Strategic Business Units (SBUs) within a market and possible open venues for strategic action. The concept was widely applied within American corporations and found its way to a sizable number of corporations elsewhere.

The adapted portfolio analysis resorted to in the following analysis continues to operate with the two identified parameters of the original concept, i.e. the relative market share and the rate of industry growth. Adjustments were, however, introduced and these touched upon the parameters as well as some derivative issues. A Strategic Business Arena (SBA) was defined as a cluster of business activities with a related technology, related end user, and measurable international market. Energy, information technology, hospitality, healthcare, finance are all SBAs. Rate of market growth was viewed in terms of the average rate of growth of export trade in that specific Strategic Industrial Arena over the period of observation. The international relative market share was equated to the relationship between country exports of products manufactured by the Strategic Business Arena and the exports of that specific product by a judgmental market leader, over the same period of time. This market leader is, by definition, another country competing in the same international market segment.

Positions within the portfolio fall into four categories. A combination of low relative market share and low rate of market growth leads to a "stability" area or an area where SBAs are distinguished with stability. High relative market share and low rate of market growth are tantamount to a "maturity" area or an area where SBAs are mature. High relative market share combined with a high rate of market growth could lead to an "expansive" area or an area where the SBAs grow. And finally low relative market share combined with a high rate of market growth connotes a "threshold" area or an area where SBAs are in an entry mode.

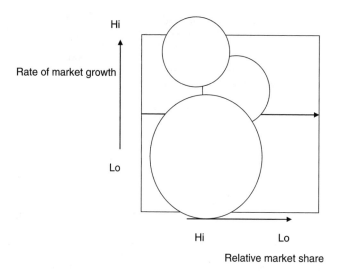

Relative market share

Figure 2.4   The strategic positioning of SBAs in a market

Flow from one area to the other differs according to country strategies and conditions in the international market. Earlier research focusing on the newly industrialized countries of South and East Asia reflected a tendency to move from an expansion to a maturity state and from maturity to stability (Figure 2.4) (El Namaki, 1989).

Libya's starting position

Libya's starting position combines the good and the bad (Tables 2.6 and 2.7). On the one hand Libya is the wealthiest country in North Africa with an enviable equitable distribution of wealth. Its economy is also externally oriented with trade as a major medium of growth. Exports, by the very nature of the resource endowment of the country, are heavy contributors (48% in 2002). The same goes for imports. On the other hand, this high wealth does not seem to translate into higher productivity whether in terms of level of productive employment;, outside the oil and gas sector, labor productivity is particularly low. This effectively separates the economy into a high value, low employment sector and a low value, high employment sector. Oil does account for a near 60 percent of GDP but contributes 3 percent to employment. This may also highlight the very high dependence on the energy sector and the infant stage of other potential sectors or areas of economic activity (Business Week, 2007).

Table 2.6 Foreign trade as a percentage of Libya's GDP for the year 2002

Item	2000
Exports of goods and services (% of GDP)	35.0
Imports of goods and services (% of GDP)	15.2

Source: World Bank data base 2006

Table 2.7 Export volume and the associated rate of market growth, Libya and the World

Year	2001	2002	2003	2004	Rate of growth per year %
Libya	987.6	983.6	1,126.5	1284.5	6.4
World	38,183.6	37,574.6	39,723.5	42,692.2	2.7

Source: International Energy Agency 2006

Libya's position in the oil industry tells a different story. First, the country has a relative market share of 0.16 (the relationship between country exports and exports of the market leader, i.e. Saudi Arabia). This is a strong position but certainly not as strong as that of ten others (Libya is number 11 in sequence, see Table 2.8). The picture gets more complex if one is to look at the reserves (Table 2.9). Libya reserves rank 8th on a global scale, way below those of, of course, Saudi Arabia and the United Arab Emirates (Figure 2.5).

The energy sector faces a broad range of challenges. A considerable increase in funding is required for upstream oil and gas activities if the sector has to optimize its output and remain a key source of wealth. Oil field and oil discoveries are slow and a continuation of this pace could lead to a major decline in production levels in the near future. Libya has the potential to raise oil production to above 3 mbd and this is only feasible through a considerable increase in investment.

Libya's possible future SBAs and their strategic positioning

Given Libya's strategic profile sketched above, it is the author's contention that a strategic position of Libya in the international market should be

Table 2.8 The relative market share of oil exporters in 2005*

Country	Net oil exports (million barrels per day)	The relative market share (country exports/exports of market leader)
1. Saudi Arabia	9.1	1.00
2. Russia	6.7	0.74
3. Norway	2.7	0.30
4. Iran	2.6	0.29
5. United Arab Emirates	2.4	0.26
6. Nigeria	2.3	0.25
7. Kuwait	2.3	0.25
8. Venezuela	2.2	0.24
9. Algeria	1.8	0.20
10. Mexico	1.7	0.19
11. Libya	1.5	0.16
12. Iraq	1.3	0.14
13. Angola	1.2	0.13
14. Kazakhstan	1.1	0.12
15. Qatar	1.0	0.11

Notes: * Table includes all countries with net exports exceeding 1 million barrels per day in 2005

Source: Oil export data derived from OPEC data base

Table 2.9 World oil reserves by country, Jan 2006

Country	Reserve level in million of barrels
1. Saudi Arabia	264.3
2. Canada	178.8
3. Iran	132.5
4. Kuwait	115.0
5. UAE	101.5
6. Venezuela	97.8
7. Russia	79.7
8. Libya	60.0
9. Nigeria	39.1
10. United States	35.9

Source: International Energy Outlook, 2006

based on its attainment of a substantial relative market share in two prime strategic business arenas: one is energy and the other is services. Energy-related business arena should cover oil and gas, petrochemicals as well as alternative energy. Service-related businesses could relate to tourism.

Rate of market growth

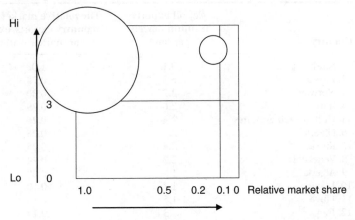

Figure 2.5   An approximation of the strategic position of Libya and Saudi Arabia in the global oil market, 2005*

Note: * Saudi Arabia is the market leader with a 1.0 coefficient. Libya is a fraction of this 1.0 or 0.16. Figure is based on export volume in 2005 (see Table 2.8). Average rate of global market growth was over the period 2001 to 2004: 2.7%. A market share below the 0.1 is considered low. The size of the circle is a function of the volume of exports

The energy SBA

Energy SBAs are and could be, in the longer term, the most productive in Libya. The sector could grow considerably and that would include both oil and gas. Gas production could actually grow to the extent of covering domestic demand and allowing for comfortable exports. The constraint here is investment, as additional money is needed for a substantial upstream oil and gas output expansion. This is a must if the sector is to deliver and continue to be the prime source of revenue and wealth for the country. The current situation could be described as suboptimal with production constraints within existing fields, slow discoveries, and lack of integrated gas projects. There is also a need to restructure the sector especially with an eye on the decision making processes and the role assigned to the different players. An unclear relationship between the government and the respective state agencies undermines the potential for future adjustment. Absence also of key business information that hampers planning is yet another bottleneck.

There are opportunities for growth and diversification in petrochemicals too. Refining capacity upgrading should balance output with domestic demand for oil products. Natural gas should replace diesel as the fuel. Access to a large, low cost resource base of attractively priced NLG offers the prospect of a strong competitive position in the global chemicals sector. Libya's low cost feedstock may also prove to provide a comparative advantage especially if combined with the logistical advantages of the country.

Alternative energy or more specifically solar energy is an unexplored business area in Libya though it could, on the face of it, provide a rich potential.

The tourism SBA

Tourism would be the second SBA with a potential in Libya. Tourism generates employment, contributes to infrastructure, and transfers skills and know-how to the local market. The point of infrastructure is significant given its visible impact on roads, airports, and all other means of physical and nonphysical communications. It also has a high value added impact. The problem is the competitive environment of tourism. With formidable neighbors in Tunisia to the West and Egypt to the East, Libya has to work hard to establish a position. What Libya could claim as an advantage over those two competitors is the clean environment, the lower cost, and different historical landmarks.

Figure 2.6 projects the possible positioning of the two SBAs within a ten year time span. The energy SBA would take a more dominant position that that of today with increased output and greater exports enhancing relative market shares, while rate of market growth is sustained at the current level. As to the tourism SBA, there exists a possibility that this could become a major drive with sizeable market share in the Mediterranean and an accelerating rate of market growth as well. Both projections are based on investment stimulation in the two sectors and elimination of the constraints referred to earlier.

Summary and conclusions

Libya has maintained a socialist economy where the government is the main player. The government owns major assets, provides employment, sponsors economic initiatives, and supports social programs. Libya's economic growth has been constrained by adverse global political

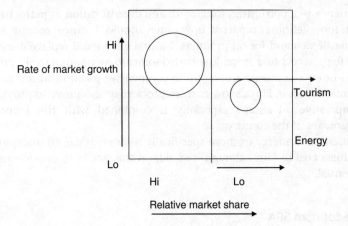

Figure 2.6 Proposed future positioning of the Libyan energy and tourism SBAs within the Mediterranean tourism market*

Note: * The location of the circle is a function of the potential contribution of tourism in Libya to the total Mediterranean market. It does not reflect the size of demand. The time dimension is variable depending on the consistency of the measures and effectiveness of application

currents, a situation that is changing very rapidly. Future economic growth strategy and where the country will go from today's favorable position is the question addressed by this chapter. Analysis followed a quasi BCG model where a country's position in the global market is identified with a number of SBAs where the country has a strategic advantage. This analysis of Libya's current economic and business conditions leads to the unmistakable conclusion that the energy industry is the major player and prime source of revenue and wealth. A single SBA or area of economic and technological strength was chosen by the country as the prime vehicle for economic growth. Are there other SBAs? The answer is yes. The energy industry could be further developed downstream and investment in a petrochemical industry could pay. Nonenergy SBAs could focus on tourism and the integration of Libya into the network of tourist hubs that the Mediterranean offers.

3
Corporate Strategic Thinking

3.1   Emirates pursuing: Is it the right strategy?

The problem

The airline industry is a volatile industry plagued with excessive losses, restructuring, and bankruptcies. There is a long history of bailout packages in the United States, and efficiency seeking mergers in Europe. The industry is cyclical. Four or five years of poor performance proceed five or six years of improved performance. But profitability in the good years is generally low, in the range of 2–3 percent (net profit). In times of profit, airlines lease new generations of airplanes and upgrade services in response to higher demand. As in many mature industries, consolidation is a trend though the shape may differ. Airline groupings may consist of limited bilateral partnerships, long-term, multi-faceted alliances between carriers, equity arrangements, mergers, or takeovers. Since governments often restrict ownership and mergers between companies in different countries, most consolidation takes place within a country.

The Middle East market demonstrates these weakness and more. Events such as September 11 and the Iraq conflict, the conflict in Lebanon, uncertainty in Palestine and many other parts of the region introduce a strong element of turbulence. Emirates was born within this turbulent environment and grew under the same unstable conditions. It has, however, demonstrated an ability to grow despite this hostile environment. Moreover, it has been able to evolve a global strategy that took it beyond the limits of the regional market. It has been working towards a vision (*New Nation* online, May 2006).

The following case explores Emirates' rise to its current level and questions present day strategies of the airline and whether these are sustainable in the longer term.

The competitive profile of Emirates

Emirates Airlines is the product of a search for effective key drivers for the Dubai economy. It belongs to a package that includes air transportation, tourism, hospitality, and real estate. Lack of oil resources and search for alternative sources of economic growth induced the Dubai government to embark upon this search. The launch of the airline came in 1985 with the Dubai government as the sole owner and the sole investor. Early services extended to 60 destinations in 42 countries throughout Europe, Middle East, Far East, Africa, Asia, and Australia. Early strategies stressed quality in product, equipment, organization, and services. A multinational crew was recruited, a modern fleet purchased, and an overall quality image was promoted. The airline took off and managed within a fairly short time to expand routes, achieve high returns, boost technology, and enter new markets.

Emirates' entry into new markets was based on the notion that Emirates is a global airline based in the Middle East and not an Arab airline operating abroad! This has induced established carriers in Europe and Australia, such as Air France, KLM, British Airways, Lufthansa, and Qantas, to perceive Emirates' strategic positioning as a global carrier and thus as a major threat. These carriers found it difficult to deal with Emirates competitive cost advantage. Some of them, such as Air France and Qantas, openly accused Emirates of receiving hidden state subsidies and of maintaining a too cozy relationship with Dubai's airport authority as well as its aviation authority, both wholly state-owned entities. In addition, they have also accused Emirates of taking unfair advantage of its government shareholder's sovereign borrower status. They claim that this masks its true financial performance and reduces its borrowing costs to below market rates (*The Economist* October 5, 2006; the *Financial Times* July 19, 2006).

Emirates competes directly with a near twenty three airlines operating in sixteen countries in the Middle East. They all share the need for good management and cost reduction especially when it comes to major cost items such as taxation, security, insurance, and fuel. A major competitor in the Gulf area is Gulf Air, a partly government owned airline (government of Abu Dhabi) with strong support and a wide network. Gulf posed a serious threat to Emirates thanks to the so-called open skies policy, a policy that allows free access to Dubai airport and minimal entry restrictions. Yet profitability histories of both airlines diverge strongly. At a time when Gulf is facing negative results and is compelled to cut routes, Emirates is experiencing one cycle of expansion after another.

Emirates has a fairly young fleet. The average age is 5.4 years (February 2007). Favorable terms offered by both Airbus and Boeing during the post Sept 11 era encouraged the airline to embark upon a massive acquisition swing that included up to 150 long-haul wide-bodied jets. This order will make Emirates the world's largest 777 operator. Global aspiration undoubtedly stood at the heart of this decision. "By the end of the financial year (2005–2006) we had a fleet of 91 aircraft, serving 83 destinations carrying 14.5 million passengers and one million tonnes of freight. By 2010 we will have 156 aircraft serving 101 destinations, carrying an estimated 26 million passengers per year. Such is the projected growth of Emirates" (Emirates Annual Report 2005–2006).

Emirates had and continues to have its share of glitter. It received the prestigious airline of the year award for the first time in 2001 and repeated the feat in 2002. It was also named, in 2007, the UAE's top brand among 25 other local firms. It has a base value of US$ 6.3 billion. Emirates was also labeled by some industry executives as " … one of the region's most forward-thinking and innovative organizations in the area of technology" for its acquisition of "the most innovative storage infrastructures in the Middle East." Emirates, finally, has also begun construction of its own luxury five star hotel and towers. And 2007 will witness the introduction of a docking capability for Apple Computer's iPod portable music and video player in Emirates fleet (*Wall Street Journal*, Nov 2006).

Marketing expenses account for a far greater share of its total costs than for most of its competitors (*The Economist*, Oct 2006).

The business model

Emirates business model is based on the following premises:

• **Labor Cost Economies**: A mix of Emirates lean workforce and young fleet account for its remarkable low cost and a strong cost-based competitive profile. The labor triggered low cost is created by a very lean workforce, comparable to the leading low-cost "no frills" airlines rather than other traditional "flag carriers." This, along with a simpler organizational structure, allows the airline to minimize overheads. Its low cost base is according to some industry analysts second only to Ryan air on a cash cost per seat basis.

- **Toothless Workforce**: Emirates workforce is not unionized.
- **Government Blithe Support**: Emirates received and continues to receive direct and indirect financial and nonfinancial support from the Dubai government.
- **Fleet Cost Economies**: Emirates airlines operate an all-wide-body fleet resulting in lower unit costs compared with airlines operating mixed narrow/wide-body fleets. This enables Emirates to use these aircraft's cargo capacity to boost its overall revenues and total profits, especially at times when the passenger business passes through a seasonal trough or when an economic downturn adversely impacts the passenger numbers. Its Dubai hub also allows it to take advantage of increasing cargo business between China, India, and West Africa.
- **Strategic Distance**! Emirates has so far refused to join any of the major global airline alliances and questions the advantages such alliances bring for the airlines as well as their customers, especially after taking into consideration the high costs of compliance with alliance membership.
- **Opportunistic Strategies**: Emirates strategic behavior can best be described as proactive and at times, opportunistic. Market segment gaps are sought and filled with speed. Price differentiation is strong.
- **Well Positioned Hub**: Dubai airport is an excellent hub that allows Emirates airlines to profitably serve secondary destinations as well as connect such places via its global Dubai hub (*The Economist* October 6, 2006).

The strategies

Emirates' strategies are a function of the environment where it operates and the product of intrinsic strategic thinking from within the carrier. The environment could be viewed in terms of Porter's five forces, i.e. threat of entrants, power of suppliers, power of buyers, substitution effect, and rivalry:

- Threat of New Entrants. It seems, to all appearances, that the airline industry is a low entry barrier industry. Finance, the prime entry barrier, is readily available in the Middle East and technology and expertise are purchasable.
- Power of Suppliers. Boeing and Airbus are the two main suppliers and competition among them is probable, observable, but not abominable! Also, the likelihood of a supplier integrating vertically isn't very likely.

- Power of Buyers. The bargaining power of airline industry buyers in the Middle East is quite low.
- Availability of Substitutes. Threat is really limited given the distances in the Middle East, and the fast pace that is becoming a symbol of the area.
- Competitive Rivalry. The airline industry is generally highly competitive and highly competitive industries generally, again, earn low returns because the cost of competition is high. This can spell disaster in low cycle times. The Middle East, however, provides a different story thanks to governments' readiness to cushion the shocks and help the flag carrier go on flag carrying!

So the environment carries the threat of new entrants and competitive rivalry but not a real threat from substitution or buyers and suppliers for that matter.

Emirates' strategic behavior, within this kind of environment, runs parallel to Ansoff's product market strategies Matrix. Actually the parallel is so close that one supposes that top management or those responsible for the strategy formulation function within the corporation have been working with this model in the back of their minds. Emirates' strategies included penetration strategies, product development strategies, market development strategies, and even a recent element of diversification. Let us examine these (Figure 3.1).

- Market penetration. The Middle East is Emirates' prime market segment and the segment that justified the creation of the company in the first place. This market is being thoroughly penetrated by Emirates as a deliberate policy.

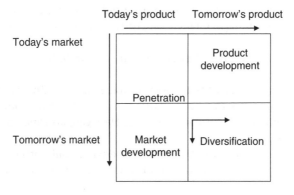

Figure 3.1   Emirates strategic behavior

- Product development: Emirates product development is of modest proportion. It is related to product specifications and the type of services offered more than the introduction of changes in product mix.
- Market development: Emirates geographic expansion, including entry into the United States market, is a typical example of market development.
- Diversification: Emirates' entry into the storage market is another example of diversification.

Is Emirates effective? or unique?

There is little doubt that Emirates strategies are effective. Results attest to that. Not only in terms of revenue, asset, and capital expenditure, performance has improved over time, but also other measures of performance. Emirates Airline's revenues totaled AED 22.7 (US$6.3 billion) for the year 2006 or 27 percent above 2005 level. Passenger seat factor also reached 75.9 percent, 1.3 percent above 2005 level. And capacity increased to 15,803 million ton-kilometers. Breakeven load factor remained relatively low at 60.3 percent, and yield improved for the fourth consecutive year, to US0.55 cents per Revenue ton-kilometers. Introducing the 2006 annual report, the Chairman said:

> These results clearly show that Emirates' customer-oriented approach and investments in providing a quality product – the best aircraft that money can buy; top-flight service, and travel experience at a competitive price – has paid off in terms of retaining and winning new customers globally ... It has been another tough year with pressure from fuel costs continuously dampening our robust net income production. Emirates has returned its 18th consecutive annual profit, and we are pleased to have achieved this solid performance while expanding our operations in an increasingly competitive environment.

There are strategic flaws, though. They boil down to the following:

- Is Emirates really the product of Arab strategic thinking? Emirates is managed by a board whose chairman is Sheikh Ahmed bin Saeed Al Maktoum and Vice chairman is Maurice Flanagan, an expatriate, who is also a President of Emirates Group. While there is little doubt that the broad strokes are Sheik El Maktoum's, there is equally little doubt that Mr Flanagan is the strategic steward and the prime decision maker

Table 3.1 Emirates performance 2005, 2006

Variable	Passenger		Cargo		Others		Total	
	2005	2006	2005	2006	2005	2006	2005	2006
2006 Revenue	13.8	17.5	3.5	4.5	0.6	0.7	17.9	22.7
Total assets	23.0	30.5	0.06	0.3	0.6	0.6	23.7	31.3
Capital expenditure	3.0	4.4	0.06	0.2	0.05	0.2	3.2	4.7

Source: Emirates Group Annual Report 2005–2006

within the airline. " ... While there is no pressure from his employers to retire, Flanagan, who is 77, explains that there is a succession plan in place. The carrier has a program to bring along UAE nationals, and eventually a local will run the show. But there are no targets or timescales ... Flanagan himself shows no sign of slowing down, nor is there any dimming in his enthusiasm for the carrier ... " (*Airline Business* November 16, 2006).

Key vice presidents of the airline are all expatriate executives too. Those include the President of Emirates Airlines, the President of the Group Support Services, and the President of Danata and associated companies.

- Is Emirates' disregard for the rising regional competition strategically opportune? Competition is on the horizon. Etihad Airways, a government of Abu Dhabi creation, is coming up with a different approach to regional and international travel in stark contrast with Emirates. In contrast to the low-cost airlines, Etihad is focusing on offering a product that appeals to travelers who want a premium service, at a competitive international price. Key to the Etihad's promise is the move away from the traditional classes, as it becomes the first regional airline to take the concept of premium economy and rework it for the regional marketplace.

Etihad refers to passengers as guests and has guest zones rather than fare classes. The three zones – Diamond, Pearl, and Coral – do not correspond directly to first, business, and economy classes.

Etihad is a potent rival working hard to change critical product features. Is Emirates able to meet this challenge?

- How far can a cost cutting strategy go? Emirates is under cost pressure. Fuel costs remained the top expenditure in 2006 accounting for 27.2 percent of total operating costs, up from 21.4 percent the previous year. Like other airlines, Emirates was forced to increase the fuel surcharge component of the fare, which only covered 41% of incremental costs (*New Nation*, May 20, 2006). This could lead to the question of how far a cost cutting strategy can go given the very lean staff and the sharp eye that the airline holds on other cost items.

- Why buy, why not integrate backwards? Emirates has been embarking upon a massive buying swing that will inflate the size of its fleet and expand capacity. The volume of investment is sizable and the strategic implications are far-reaching. The strategic question that could be posed here is why buy, why not integrate backwards? Put differently, why not acquire equity in the aircraft building industry? Qatar is flirting with the idea. It may even be more than flirting, but what is wrong with that? They seem to be following the right track. Shareholding in Airbus or Boeing will have obvious long-term advantages and may even transform the fortunes of Emirates altogether.

- Is it strategic growth or a windfall? Emirates growth is impressive by any measure but is it genuine or just a by-product of Dubai's own economic upsurge. One can entertain the notion that the airline's growth was largely a windfall from Dubai's economic bonanza. After all a GDP rate of growth of 8% for the UAE as a whole, and figures near that in earlier years, has a spill over. And if tourism is one of the drivers of this growth, that spill over is very likely to reflect on the prime air carriers within the region.

- Is there not a risk in shunning strategic alliances? Strategic alliance is a theme that dominated the airline industry for decades. It is rather surprising, therefore, that Emirates shuns this strategy at both regional and global level! Arguments for this evasion are not spelled out in the airline's documents and ulterior motives may not be ruled out. The issue remains, however, that alliances within the airline industry have their justifications and benefits and an alliance aversion may not work to the advantage of Emirates in the longer term.

- Is Emirates' fleet composition congruent with market needs? Airline fleets are usually built around a mix of profiles and capacities. The mix is between international carriers, or 130+ seat planes that have the ability to take passengers just about anywhere in the world producing a company revenue of US$1 billion or more; national airlines seating 100–150 people and have revenues between US$100 million and US$1 billion; regional companies with revenues of less than US$100 million that focus on short-haul flights, and cargo airlines whose main purpose is to transport goods and whose revenues are well below the US$100 million mark.

Emirates has strategically positioned itself, market wise, in the first and third category and technology wise, in the first. Whether this is strategically and operationally opportune remains to be seen.

Summary and conclusions

The airline industry is a volatile industry plagued with excessive losses, restructuring, and bankruptcies. There is a long history of bailout packages in the United States, and efficiency seeking mergers in Europe. The industry is cyclical with strong revenue, asset, and profitability shifts. The Middle East market demonstrates these weakness and more. Emirates Airlines has managed, despite this unusual environment, to grow and prosper. It became a global airline that is based in the Middle East and not an Arab airline operating abroad! Not only revenue, assets, and capital expenditure improved over time, but also other performance measures as passenger seat factor and break even payload. A strategy of market penetration, product development, and market development worked well for the airline. This was not only the outcome of Dubai's overall growth strategy but also specific strategies pursued by the airline. Points of weakness within this very positive picture could relate to the extent to which the adopted strategies are really the result of Arab thinking and Arab management, the limits of the cost cutting strategy pursued by the airline, the prudence of buying instead of integrating backward, the wisdom of shunning alliances, and the asset composition framework maintained by the airline today.

3.2   Does SABIC have the right vision?

The problem

SABIC or Saudi Basic Industries Corporation is a company with a vision. It puts that forward in statements, publications, interviews, and declarations. A vision that is rooted in Saudi Arabia's pivotal position within the energy industry and its unusual dominance of the global energy markets. SABIC was created in 1976 to add value to Saudi Arabia's natural hydrocarbon resources and grew, over time, to become a leading global petrochemical company. Revenues, geographical spread, and

Table 3.2   SABIC key performance parameters 2004

Performance parameter	2004
Sales	SR 78.3 billion (US$20.9)
Gross profit	SR 33.1 billion (US$8.8)
Shareholder equity	SR 62.0 billion (US$16.5 billion)
Total assets (SR billion)	SR 137.0 billion (US$36.5)

Source: SABIC Annual Report 2005

product diversity attest to that. The government of Saudi Arabia owns 70 percent of SABIC's assets while the other 30 percent is owned by private shareholders in both Saudi Arabia and the GCC States (Gulf Cooperation Council countries).

SABIC has a wide product range covering basic chemicals, intermediates, industrial polymers, fertilizers, and metals. It is the world's third polyethylene producer and fourth polypropylene producer. SABIC is also the world's single largest producer and exporter of granular urea fertilizer (SABIC Annual Report, 2005) (Table 3.2).

SABIC has a solid track record and is considered healthy and competitive by domestic and international standards. The question could arise, however, whether SABIC's growth scenarios are organic or driven by a vision? And if it is a matter of vision, how realistic is vision at a time when capacity is expanded throughout the Middle East and is moving closer to the final consumer in the Far East? These are the questions that we will address in this section. There are arguments for both. The petrochemical industry is a growth industry *par excellence*. Global economic growth drives demand for petrochemicals and petrochemicals are the prime requisite for economic growth. Yet one needs more than demand driven growth in order to grow and prosper. A corporation the size and scope of SABIC needs a vision, a sense of direction, a desired state at the end of the tunnel. Does SABIC have that?

Who is SABIC?

SABIC is the tenth largest petrochemical company in the world and the largest nonoil company in Arab countries. It operates from a base in Riyadh with manufacturing facilities in both the east and west of the kingdom. Altogether there are 17 world-class manufacturing affiliates in Saudi Arabia, mainly in Al-Jubail on the Arabian Gulf coast and Yanbu on the Red Sea coast. European facilities were acquired (from the Dutch petrochemical corporation DSM) in early 2000. These facilities, in Geleen (The Netherlands) and Gelsenkirchen (Germany), produce and market polypropylene, polyethylene, and other hydrocarbons. SABIC has an interest in three regional ventures based in Bahrain. And is also taking a large step with Jubail United Petrochemical Co., which it is building alone. The venture will bring 1 million metric tons of ethylene plus ethylene glycol and α-olefins to the market.

SABIC is a strong company with blue chip global credentials. It has been ranked by Bloomberg as the thirteenth largest company in the world by market capitalization. It was also ranked as the second largest company outside the United States and the UK by market value. The company was judged to be the best manufacturing company in the Middle East in 2005.

SABIC has been faring well, financially. Revenue and returns reached record levels in recent years. Gross profit amounted to SR 33.1 billion (US$8.8 billion) in 2004 and revenues reached SR 78.30 billion (US$20.8 billion) in the same year. Profit increase averaged 58 percent over the five years ending in 2004 and sales growth averaged 25 percent over the same period. The company's total assets stood at SR 137 billion (US$36.5 billion) at the end of 2004 and total shareholder equity amounted to SR 62.0 billion (US$16.5) also in 2004.

SABIC is organized along SBU (Strategic Business Units) lines. There are six of those: basic chemicals; intermediates; polyolefins; PVC and polyester; fertilizers, and metals. Basic chemicals is largest and the most dominant among the six SBUs. A shared services organization provides common services across the corporation. The corporate core consists of Human Resources, Corporate Finance, Corporate Control, and Research and Technology.

SABIC, the global petrochemical industry and the Middle East

The petrochemical industry is a dynamic if not volatile industry! The industry faces several challenges (Al-Mady, 2007):

- **Constrained international flows. The** Doha Round is critical to the flow of petrochemical trade yet the round is surrounded by challenges and the outlook is blurred. Global petrochemical products producers rely on access to global markets.
- **Global warming and the inherent threat to consumption.** As the petrochemical industry depends heavily upon utilization of

hydrocarbons and fuel, it cannot ignore global warming. Target CO_2 emissions and establishing carbon trading regimes. At some point, efforts to reduce CO_2 emissions are likely to impact the industry.

* **EU's protective measures: the "Reach" program**. The EU has adopted a program called "REACH" or Registration, Evaluations, and Authorization of Chemicals program. "REACH" comes into force in June 2007 and will require pre-registration of thousands of chemicals by January 1, 2009. This will impact all producers who manufacture chemicals in the EU as well as those who export chemicals into the EU. While this program is currently confined to the EU, it is likely to spread to other regions.

* **Geopolitics**. The petrochemical industry, and its inputs, concentrates, to a large extent in the Middle East, an area not known for sedate existence.

Add to that developments in China, India, and the United States and the picture gets more complex. China and India are lands or rising demand. China's developing absorption capacity will make it the primary petrochemical market for some time to come. It has its own supplies and is working at an increase in those domestic supplies but demand outstrips these supplies by a long way. India is in a more or less similar situation. The United States provides an opposite scenario.

Where does Saudi Arabia stand in the middle of it all?

One way to consider the Saudi position is to examine Saudi Arabia's competitive advantage and whether this could be sustained in the long term. An attempt to assess that was done (Jasimuddin, 2001) by applying Porter's competitive strategy (Porter, 1980). The model identified five forces of possible impact on competitive positioning and they include new entrants, bargaining powers of buyers, bargaining power of suppliers, substitutes, and, finally, rivalry among operators within the same industry. The result was the identification of several points of strength that the Saudi economy has and could provide protection. These included the banking sector which is considered strong and not susceptible to negative influences triggered by external, global financial currents. And labor-management relations based on the illegality of labor unions and the absence of a minimum wage. There is no labor unrest in the kingdom. A near 80 percent of the total labor force in the kingdom is non-Saudis.

Summarizing, the global petrochemical industry is at the crossroads. A decade ago the US was the most competitive place in the world to produce base chemicals, Europe was fairly competitive, and Saudi Arabia's competitive advantage rested with the raw material. Saudi infrastructure was fragile and could not sustain an upsurge in output or foreign market entry. However, today the picture has changed. North America has lost considerable competitiveness, Europe remains constant, and Saudi Arabia or SABIC has gained advantage and changed the global competitive landscape for base chemicals. The situation is bound to change again, in the course of the next decade (*Arab News*, 2006). Yet SABIC's outlook depends on three determinants: political stability (or instability) in the Middle East, raw material supply, and logistics. Instability is abundant in the Middle East and, as we said earlier, it could have far-reaching impact on supplies and growth scenarios. The feed stocks aren't unlimited either. A price increase is bound to reflect those scarcities of supply as well as the increase in cost of extraction. Logistics are an issue because of fairly low cost of sea transportation prevailing now. A sizeable increase in production and shipments is bound to stimulate capacity bottlenecks and price hikes.

SABIC's vision and strategies

SABIC's official publications deal with the issue of vision by making a distinction between "aims", "values," and "standards". It describes the aim as " ... to become the world's preferred manufacturer and marketer of chemical and metal products." It goes on to describe the values as a commitment to develop " ... the country's natural resources and to improving the skills and education of its people ... respect Saudi cultural values. Respect the values of every country in which we work." And it deals with standards as using " ... natural resources and human talent to their best advantage by innovating, educating, and using the latest technology." SABIC's publications describe the company as " ... the largest and most reliably profitable public company in the Middle East." And attributes this state to three drivers: investment in local partnerships, superior research and technology, and an ambitious global growth strategy. It effectively says what is said elsewhere

> ... for **Saudi Arabia** to effectively capitalize on its petrochemical potential, and production cost advantage, it must take a global view and become a world player – and that means looking for opportunities outside the **Middle East**.
> Within SABIC we are engaged in a process of redefining our businesses and our business strategies. Within Saudi Arabia, we are

helping to build new learning and caring communities. Externally, we are inventing new markets with new alliances and partnerships. (*World Economic Forum*, interview with Mohamed Al-Mady, CEO, SABIC, 2006)

What this boils down to is diversifying the product portfolio, establishing more joint ventures with industry majors, placing greater emphasis on research and development, and diversifying further downstream.

The SABIC vision is to be A Shared Services Organization that provides common services across the SABIC business in the kingdom. The corporate core consists of leading global Human Resources; Corporate Finance; Corporate Control and manufacturer, and Research and Technology (R&T).

SABIC's management puts the vision issue within the following framework. "At SABIC, our vision is clear. We will be a leading global manufacturer and marketer of hydrocarbon and metal products. We are committed to growing and expanding in ways that support our customers' needs ... anywhere in the world." And it translates this vision into a strategy that spells out looking beyond its region for its competitive advantage, both in terms of cost and market responsiveness. It is important to have a global reach and SABIC's acquisition of DSM's and Huntsman's petrochemical assets is an indication of this approach and is intended to prevent overexposure to a single geographic manufacturing site. "In addition, this provides a sound platform for further organic growth" Further, alternatives to traditional feedstocks must be found. For some of these we will rely on exploration for new sources but it is also an area in which technology has an important role to play.

Is it the right vision? are they the right strategies?

To be able to answer this question we have to look at the future of things to be, i.e. the outlook for the petrochemical industry. In the longer term, emerging economies will have a major impact on the petrochemical industry and the future markets for petrochemicals. New economic powers are evolving with economic strength of their own. China, India, Russia, Brazil, and Mexico are becoming strong engines of economic growth triggering a shift in consumption patterns of petrochemicals. It is estimated that by the year 2025, emerging economies will account for over 60 percent of total world GDP (measured as purchasing power parity). The future of the global petrochemical industry will be closely intertwined with these developments within the emerging economies of the world.

We can pose, in the light of these developments, a few questions with regards to the vision and strategies outlined above.

Where to go down stream

SABIC's acquisitions so far have taken place in the Netherlands and in the United States. The question could arise, however, where to place these acquisitions and under what conditions. The US seems to be a logical destination but there are those who think that it would not make good business sense for SABIC to acquire base chemical assets in the US itself because of the long-term viability of such investments and because North America is price volatile and has high raw material costs. SABIC would better, then, export to North America and to Europe from its European operations instead of establishing a base there (*Arab News*, 2006).

Are base chemicals the answer?

The outlook for base chemicals is excellent according to industry forecasts. Massive demand and expanding capacities are providing a benign scenario.

> The winners at the end of the day are those companies who have economies of scale and those who have raw material advantage and engineering and management expertise. SABIC is one of those few companies that have all three, raw materials, management, and engineering. It is well positioned to dominate this market for many years to come. (*Arab News*, 2006)

Is this the way management see it? Is not the pace too careful?

Is Saudi petrochemicals' competitive advantage real?

Saudi Arabia is endowed with resources, physical and monetary. The economic success of Saudi Arabia is built in part on its comparative advantages and on overcoming its disadvantages. Although the government strongly supports a free market economy based on competition, Saudi Arabia is ranked low in global competitiveness. Several factors contribute to this low ranking and the question is: in what way will those less than optimum variables influence the realization of SABIC's ambitious vision?

The issue of size

Companies in the commodity or basic petrochemical industry must demonstrate economies of scale before being able to play a key role on a global scale. A globalization strategy is, to a very large extent, a function of this scale. And the scale is large, dictated by the size of manufacturing plants, capital needs, technology input, management skill demands, work force skill requirements, global supply chain lines, etc. Has SABIC reached that scale? Is it ready for threshold?

Summary and conclusions

SABIC is a company with a vision that is rooted in Saudi Arabia's pivotal position within the energy industry and its unusual dominance of the global energy market. SABIC has a solid track record and is considered healthy and competitive by domestic and international standards. The question could arise, however, whether SABIC's growth scenarios are organic or driven by a vision? And if it is a matter of vision, how realistic is this vision? SABIC vision is clear; it is to be a leading global manufacturer and marketer of hydrocarbon and metal products. The petrochemical industry is, however, a dynamic if not volatile industry! It faces several challenges too. The political stability (or instability) in the Middle East, raw material supply, and logistics are some of these. Will SABIC fulfill the vision? It depends on several variables: where to go downstream; are basic chemicals the answer; is Saudi competitive advantage real; what are the limitations of size.

3.3   Misr Spinning and Weaving – Strategic control too little too late!

The problem

Strategy formulation and implementation is a waste if there is no strategic control. Massive energies put into environmental scanning, the old and tired SWOT, the search for strategic moves and the management of change is all wasted if there is no strategic control. Yet this is exactly what many companies do today. They allot considerable resources to "where we plan to be" instead of "where we ought to be". One does not have to go far to stumble across evidence. Polaroid's late realization that the days of film photography were numbered, Kodak's late recognition that digital photography is the future, Ford's late accommodation of the structural changes in the automotive industry, and, DSM of the Netherlands' late move into 'fine chemicals'. All are cases where strategies focused on improving an established position instead of the search for a better "fit" within an arena.

A measure of strategic control would have taken them in the right direction.

The problem, however, is that strategic control means different things to different people. Just scan the definitions by key authors from Anthony to Kaplan, and you will reach this conclusion. Some definitions resort to the popular and others seek safety in the familiar. Some place the issue within the management control framework (Anthony, Govindarajan, 1998). Others position it within a "balanced score card" framework implying that the balanced score card provides a "strategic control system that measures efficiency, quality, innovation, and customer response" (Kaplan and Norton, 1992). Some others make it even simpler by stating that strategic control is "the process by which managers monitor the ongoing activities of an organization and its members and take corrective action to improve performance when needed" (Hill and Jones, 2004). None of these tackles the core issue of dynamic change and organization fitness within a new set of realities.

What follows is an attempt at projecting strategic control within a dynamic perspective. We discuss the conceptual framework and provide illustrative evidence from old case histories such as Polaroid and present day ones with the status of Eastman Kodak and Ford. All are cases where timely application of strategic control tests would have changed the course of events!

What is strategic control?

So, strategic control means different things to different people. It is the author's view that a clear definition would remove a lot of misunderstandings. The author's contention is that "Strategic control is a measure of the dynamic compatibility between the organization and the environment, over a foreseeable future time horizon". Strategic control could, within this framework, be exercised by measuring two variables; company attributes and environmental change over time. Strategic control relates tomorrows attributes to tomorrows evolving conditions. It recognizes the dynamic forces of change and points to measures that should be taken in order to respond to these forces (Table 3.3).

Strategic control views visions as variables with changeable attributes, over time.

Table 3.3 Strategic control versus management control

Variable	Strategic control	Management control
Time	Borderless time horizon	Vision time horizon
Core competencies	Future	Present
Roots	Environment	Benchmarks
Outcome	Potential	Achievable

How to practice strategic control

The road to strategic control goes through the concept of "fitness". An organization should "fit" within an industry, have goals that "fit" its potential, have core competencies that 'fit' new future demands, and have resources that would "fit" future dynamics. One could measure this fitness by trying to find objective answers to a number of key questions.

The "potential" fitness test

The key question here is: are your goals in line with your potential? Many goals are deduced or extrapolated and bear, in reality, little relevance to the "true" potential of the organization. The following questions may help you find an answer.

- What is the "true" revenue potential (not the forecast, extrapolated, or budgeted) of your products? How does your actual revenue compare to that potential?
- What is the "true" market share potential for your products and how far away are you from that?
- Are you exploring all possible potential-enhancing technology application opportunities accessible to the organization?
- Are there venues for (internal or external) synergy that might increase your potential?
- Would a strategic alliance enhance your potential within your industry? How many of those have you been considering in the past year? How many are "on the horizon"?

The "industry" fitness test

The key issue here is really whether you are in the right industry or not. And would you continue to be there for a foreseeable time horizon or not. Questions that may help clearing this issue would include:

- What is the rate of growth of your industry?
- At what stage are you in your industry life cycle?

- At what stage in the product life cycle are your products?
- Were there recent entrants into your industry and what was their entry strategy?
- Is your industry highly concentrated? Is there a trend towards high concentration?
- Are there major technology shifts in your industry?
- Is there major change in the technology coefficients of your products?
- What is your relative market share and did that change over time?
- Are there end-game players in the industry?

The core competency fitness test

The main question here is: do you posses a core competency and is it durable? Examining the following issues may help in providing an answer:

- What is your real core competency? Have you been testing it lately?
- How does your core competency provide a competitive edge over the longer term?
- How "durable" is your core competency? Is it subject to wear and tear?
- Are you developing other core competencies?
- Is your core competency transferable across industries?
- Are you prone to learning or de-learning?

The "resource" fitness test

Finally, the question here is do you possess the right resources for the evolving conditions. Consider the following questions:

- Is your equity input flexible enough to respond to greater demands for capital?
- Is the organization creditable enough to allow for an expansion in the debt base?
- Does your top management have the capacity, the strategic fit, and the degree of "dependability" that a change of direction may require?
- Is your middle management of the right capacity and potential for upward mobility?
- Do you have enough routes to new technology and would have the access and intrinsic generation competency.
- Is your organization culture open and liable to change if there is a high measure of change?

Projecting the outcome of each of that fitness test on a scale could lead to the following diagram. An "A" status is, obviously, ideal while any other alternative would be a source of concern Figure 3.2.

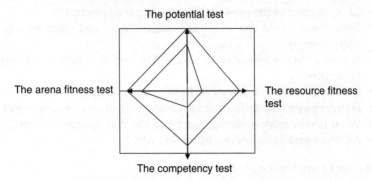

The potential test

The arena fitness test

The resource fitness test

The competency test

Figure 3.2   A possible configuration of a set strategic fitness tests

Non-Arab case illustrations

The author has opted for a number of cases all illustrative of a lapse in strategic control and insufficiency of management control measures to compensate for this lapse. The first case is Polaroid a company that very obviously failed all fitness tests. The second is Eastman Kodak a accompany that failed the potential test but is working on a remedy. The third is Ford a company that is failing the competency, the resource, and some may argue the potential fitness tests.

Polaroid

Polaroid was always fiercely protective of its innovation of instant photography, so protective that it never allowed anyone else to produce cameras compatible with its film or film compatible with itsr cameras. It also took legal action against anyone (Kodak especially) who tried to produce an instant camera. For some reason, Polaroid always won even though the basic patents on instant photography processes had long expired.

Polaroid's protectionist tactics have come home to roost. With a "mine, all mine" strategy, the company artificially limited its user base and was late in the digital photography revolution. Management was late to recognize that there is no light at the end of the tunnel for film photography.

Polaroid was not only slow but has also misled investors. Executives repeatedly blamed poor results on short-term factors, currency fluctuations, trouble in Latin America, rather than the real cause. Between

January 2000 and August 2001 Polaroid financial directors issued 'numerous misleading statements with respect to the company's financial condition' while they 'knew or should have known that this had significantly deteriorated and was much worse than represented to the public' (*Mail on Sunday*, 2004).

Polaroid's "financial restructuring" followed and bankruptcy is now a historical fact.

Applying the respective fitness tests in the late 1990s would have actually revealed Polaroid's failure on all counts!

Ford

Ford has announced a restructuring plan that would cut jobs, close facilities, reduce management layers, and re-examine products and subsidiaries! Ford is trying to reverse a 2004 loss of US$1.6 billion incurred in its North American operations. Ford earnings in 2005 of $2 billion were down 42 percent from 2004's profit of US$3.5 billion. It was the third straight year the automaker has reported a profit, but gains in Europe, Asia, and elsewhere were offset by a loss of US$1.6 billion in North American operations.

What has gone wrong at Ford and how was it not traced earlier? Ford was working with goals and strategies that were developed under familiar premises, i.e. reasonably stable industry concentration, reasonable technology shifts, and changing but predictable consumer demands. Goals suitable for that set of assumption could hurt badly if new entrants, particularly the People Republic of China, are moving fast.

Both the competencies and the potential tests of strategic control would have pointed to these dynamic forces and drew the attention to the need for response.

An Arab illustration

Misr spinning and weaving, Egypt

Misr Spinning and Weaving is one of the largest spinning and weaving companies in Egypt; its fall from grace illustrates lack of strategic control within the State enterprise sector. The company does the spinning and weaving of cotton and blended fabrics and produces ready-made garments. The demise of Misr Spinning and Weaving could be traced both to conditions within the spinning and weaving industry of Egypt, and the dynamics of the industry, and not to forget the garment industry worldwide. The following analysis explores those dynamics and positions Egypt's textile industry within that context. The specific situation of Misr Spinning and Weaving is placed at the core of the analysis.

Misr Spinning and weaving performance deteriorated, considerably, over the years. It was included, as a result, in a moribund privatization program that challenged the managerial capacities of the Egyptian government. A successful start in the mid 1990s was followed by a long-lasting stagnation. Out of 130 companies left on the privatization list, 66 are faltering concerns stuck with 160,000 employees ...

"These companies are losing billions of dollars every year and they are in need of more billions to rectify their financial situation. As many as 33 textile companies are riddled with debts and need more for restructuring and streamlining" (statement by Minister of Public Enterprise, *Al Ahram Weekly*).

Far-reaching measures are needed in this sector including modernizing production lines, raising competitive export capabilities, and drawing up new marketing strategies.

This was at a time when international competition is growing ever bolder! Hong Kong and Chinese mainland textile manufacturers are taking even greater hold of the international market. And Egypt too. But they began to pose, as time passed by, considerable challenge to the Egyptian clothing industry. This came at a time of declining performance by the Egyptian industry particularly during the 1990s when Egypt's share of the value-added end of the global textile industry (excluding China), decreased from 2.2 percent to 1.9 percent between 1990 and 2000 (UNIDO). The Egyptian clothing and textile sector seems to be ill-prepared to perform well in a quota-free global scenario. And efforts to improve the balance between the industry's strengths and its weaknesses are too little too late. And this despite the comparative advantages that the industry enjoys. Egypt has low labor costs, good geographical position, and a duty free zone system. Egyptian cotton is also considered the best in the world for its luster and length of fiber. But those strengths are contrasted with a supply chain that displays a major weakness, a dyeing and finishing sector that is underdeveloped in terms of capacity and sophistication, and weak Egyptian brands.

It goes without saying that the textile and clothing industry is of vital importance to the Egyptian economy, providing at least a million jobs. Misr Spinning & Weaving is the largest enterprise of its kind in Africa and the Middle East, employing 23,000 workers. Yet conditions there

Table 3.4 The declining export performance of the Egyptian textile and garment sectors

	1997	1998	1999	2000	2001
Product	In millions of US $				
Textiles	634.6	544.7	429.4	504.1	445.6
Garments	594.3	686.5	657.1	726.9	683.1
Total	1228.8	1231.2	1086.4	1231.1	1128.7

Source: UN statistical data base

militated against benchmark performance. Output continued to decline, inventories to rise, sales to contract, and employment to swell. And that despite a mediocre level of earnings that put the Egyptian textile workers at 8 percent of Israeli counterparts, 19 percent of Turkish counterpart, and 35 percent of Tunisian counterpart (*Al Ahram Weekly*, June 8–14, 2006).

These conditions existed for a long time and any measure of strategic control would have revealed a fitness gap, core competency gap, benchmarking gap, and potential gap!

And the situation seems to get worse. Hopes of corrective action are dim with the government announcing a legislative amendment to the executive charter of the Public Enterprises Law obliging the minister of investment to present the cabinet's economic group and the minister of manpower with the procedures for privatizing any public company, before taking any serious steps in the divestment of the company (*Al Ahram Weekly*, June 8–14, 2006). Meanwhile, Minister of Investment Mahmoud Mohieddin ruled out plans to privatize any of the state-owned spinning and weaving companies. Mohieddin revealed to the Shura Council's economic committee on a plan to restructure some of these companies, especially Misr Spinning and Weaving, which is earmarked to receive (together with another spinning and weaving public enterprise) LE1.4 billion in new investments to upgrade machinery and increase the productivity of its workers.

Summary and conclusions

Strategic control means different things to different people. This author suggests a definition that connotes dynamic compatibility between the organization and the environment, over the foreseeable time horizon.

So while traditional management controls set achievements of today against goals conceived yesterday, strategic control measures possible outcomes of tomorrow against change-induced future goals. This definition could lead to the concept of fitness. The prime building blocks of an organization should fit the environment it is living in and is evolving over a given time span. This fitness could relate to the market where the competitive fight is being conducted, the core competencies the organization has or is developing, the resources the organization can muster and the potential the organization is looking for. There should be a "test" or a measure for each of those elements of fitness. And the outcome should be yet another 'score card' telling the organization whether the strategic path it is following is conducive to the longer term vision or something else must be sought!

Here we provide non-Arab supportive evidence and an Arab case. The non-Arab cases deal with Polaroid, a company that collapsed under the weight of wrong strategies, and Ford, where symptoms of sickness left no shadow of doubt that the end is in sight.

The Arab case deals with Misr Spinning and Weaving Co, a state enterprise that, for years, showed sign of declining performance without any corrective action.

All cases highlight a lapse in strategic control. Earlier measurement of fitness and the conclusion of a gap in one of the four identified fitness domains could have triggered massive corrective action and saved the day.

4
Strategic Behavior

4.1 Is privatization the right strategy for SOEs in Egypt, Syria, and Saudi Arabia?

The problem

Privatization is a prevalent strategy made popular by the advent of free-market thinking. It is done in the name of efficiency, fiscal reward, wealth distribution, and competitiveness. Arab countries followed the trend. Household Arab corporate names, as Saudi Arabia's Saudi Telecommunication Co (STC) and Egypt's Omar Effendi, the nation's prime department store, moved into private hands. So did several other entities in a variety of Arab countries. Arab countries were, however, mild in their endorsement of this privatization strategy. The privatization efforts that began in Egypt in the late eighties, in Tunisia in the early nineties, and in Algeria in the late nineties, were, in reality, hesitant and, at times, shy. The scale was limited and the result was modest. The Egyptian program, which, by far, was the largest in the region, experienced constraints ranging from an immature capital market, especially in the early stages of the program, to innate resistance by both the bureaucracy and the unions (Jayid, 1995). These constraints did admittedly vary over time but they were there. Much of what has materialized was externally induced with the World Bank, IMF as the main levers of induction (Shirley, 1998). And the anticipated productivity, efficiency, and competitiveness outcome of the exercise are yet to be seen.

But is privatization really needed in Arab countries? Efficiency and ownership arguments are contested by the fact that a substantial number of the privatized enterprises were profit making at the time of their privatization. Saudi Telecommunication Co is an example here. The fiscal argument is undermined by the significant non-budgetary contribution of some of these public enterprises to national strategic interests. The most emphasized argument of "broadening ownership base" embraces a social objective more than an admission to private enterprise superiority.

In the next few pages I shall attempt to answer some of these questions. Analysis will be done within a number of parameters. First, it will apply to three countries: Egypt, Syria, and Saudi Arabia. These countries were chosen because they represent three stages of economic policy, the advanced transformation stage (Egypt), the early transformation stage (Syria), and the free market economy (Saudi Arabia). Second, analysis will apply to privatization strategies adopted with regards to specific public enterprises. Third, analysis will apply to the period since 1990, a period of relative change in the privatization scene of those countries.

When is privatization right?

A conceptual model

The term privatization could mean different things to different people. Most, however, agree that it applies to a transfer of ownership and control from public to private hands. This could happen through a sale of assets to private owners, a transfer of public to private ownership, a transfer of activities to private management, or a variety of those.

But is a privatization strategy appropriate under all conditions? (Goodman and Loveman, 1991).

It is the author's contention that privatization is one of several strategies open to an economy or a country. Determinants of those strategies are two: the macro-economic policies pursued by the state and the competitive position of the state enterprise or industrial sector. Externally oriented macro-economic policies, or policies emphasizing an outward orientation of the economy, require the high degree of private ownership that privatization delivers. Low relative performance of state-owned enterprises, or enterprise sectors, creates a desire for better performance and the search for ways and means of achieving that. Privatization presents itself here as a difficult to resist course of action. A blend of the two and the urge and drive towards privatization is strongest. Have both of them but with a lower attribute and the urge for privatization is less insistent.

The emerging situation is that of four alternative strategies (Figure 4.1):

- A "privatization" strategy when the external orientation is strong and competitive performance is weak. A privatization strategy would imply a transfer of either management or ownership or both to private hands.
- A "restructuring" strategy when external orientation and competitive performance are low. A restructuring strategy would imply the introduction of organizational, financial, and cultural adjustment measures changing the basic texture of the organization.
- A "retain" strategy when high enterprise performance is coupled with low external orientation of the economy. A retain strategy would imply measures inducing a continuity of the *status quo.*
- A "penetration" strategy when high enterprise performance and the external orientation of the economy are high. Penetration would imply added investment and greater market involvement.

The outward orientation of an economy today is the foundation and corner-stone of many economic policies across the globe. It spells out the level and relevance of almost all economic policy variables. It has many a root in the Structural Adjustment policies (SAPs) of the World Bank. Structural Adjustment Policies are economic policies countries must follow in order to qualify for new World Bank and International Monetary Fund (IMF) loans and make debt repayments to commercial banks, governments, and the World Bank. Although SAPs are designed for individual countries, they have common guiding principles and features which include export-led growth, privatization as well as liberal

Externally oriented economic strategies (Lo or Hi)

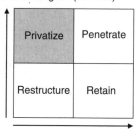

Enterprise competitive performance (Lo or Hi)

Figure 4.1   Strategic options matrix

capital flow, foreign exchange, investment, taxation, and profit repatri-
ation policies. It also requires, generally, countries to devalue their cur-
rencies against the dollar, lift import and export restrictions, balance
their budgets, and remove price controls and state subsidies (Shirley,
1998).

What it also requires, and seldom makes explicit, are managerial and
strategic competences that would support the massive shift in enterprise
structure and method of work. Also a parallel process for the introduction
of a cultural shift leading to an appreciation of free-market thinking,
acceptance of expatriate management, fluid job market conditions, and
docile trade union attitude.

External orientation policies can best be measured through a basket of
parameters. These would include:

- Exports of goods and services as percentage of GDP;
- Foreign trade as a percentage of GDP;
- Foreign Direct Investment inflow;
- Competitiveness;
- Foreign currency regime.

The second variable in the formula, the competitive condition of the
state enterprise, is efficiency parameters and an essential yardstick for a
proper productivity-based contribution of the state enterprise to overall
economic growth. Chronic public enterprise losses combined with or
produced by over-employment by the company, under-employment of
the employees, market failure, a collapsing infrastructure, and an obsolete technology are enough internal reasons to cause concern and lead
to a search for a safer haven, i.e. a privatization formula. This limited
achievement is an indication of the enterprise's failure at fulfilling a
prime function.

Relative competitive performance can best be measured, in the
author's view, through a basket of yardsticks. These could include the
relative rate of return on investment for the industry, the relative market share (in the country concerned), the contribution of the enterprise
in question to GDP, and, finally country analysis.

Egypt

The overall picture

Egypt's economic reform program, whose roots are deeply ingrained
into an IMF liberalization program that started in 1991, contained a set

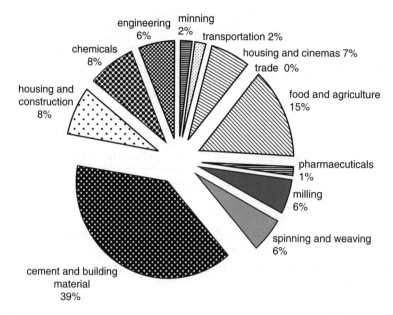

Figure 4.2 Privatization of Egypt's public enterprises in different sectors, 2000

of economic policies ensuring that market forces are given their maximum potential (Figure 4.2). A wave of restructuring and reform has continued ever since. The result was a tangible rate of economic growth and an overall air of macro-economic stability.

External orientation of the Egyptian economy

An objective measure of Egypt's external orientation could be formulated by reviewing the attributes of external orientation referred to earlier. The following table (Table 4.1) provides a summary of these attributes.

A conclusion to the external reorientation of the Egyptian economy is in focus but the road is long. Export and import contribution to GDP is way below a typical externally oriented economy. Foreign Direct Investment flow upsurge in 2004 was sudden but could mean a nudge in the right direction. Competitiveness is way below levels achieved by other emerging economies.

Egypt's conclusion of EU negotiations and the signing of the association agreement is, of course, a move in the right direction. So are also,

Table 4.1   Egypt's external orientation parameters

External orientation	Egypt	
	2003	2004
Export of goods and services	22	29
Foreign trade to GDP %	24	29
Foreign Direct Investment	0.23	2.15
Competitiveness rank	(a) Global in 2005: 52 (b) Among Arab	(a) Global in 2006: 63
Foreign currency regime	Managed currency float	

Source: World Bank Fact Sheets 2004, 2005. World Economic Forum, Global Competitiveness Report, 2006

Egypt's free trade agreements with a number of Arab countries, its agreement with the Common Market of East and South Africa (COMESA), as well as its Trade and Investment Framework Agreement (TIFA) with the United States.

Competitiveness of public enterprises in Egypt

The case of the spinning and weaving industry

Egypt has an ambitious privatization program that includes 23 state-owned enterprises in the spinning and weaving industry. The sector is out of shape and out of resources. The sector, in the words of the Minister for Industry, is "money loss making due to historical burdens of excess labor, unbalanced financial structure with huge indebtedness to banks, overinvestment and outdated technology among other factors." And this is at a time when this sector absorbs 20 percent of total public enterprise investment (June 2003 data), contributes 30 percent (or 130, 000 workers) to public enterprise labor force, contributes 35 percent of total indebtedness to the banking sector!

Also at a time when Egypt has a significant comparative advantage in cotton and the government views that this is a sector with considerable strategic significance.

The emerging strategic choice

Egypt's ambitious economic reform program has induced the government to take a proactive role in privatization. It did go a long way towards making those enterprises attractive to foreign and domestic investors alike, but the problem lies in the enterprise's mediocre performance and the failure of repeated attempts at improving this performance. This is a situation reflected in Figure 4.3 below: A low competitive performance of enterprises coupled with a strong external orientation of the economy as a whole. A remedy would require a restructuring phase that transforms the enterprise into an attractive object. Once this goal is achieved, a privatization bid could follow.

The Egyptian government seems to be following this strategy. The dyeing and spinning subsectors have undergone extensive restructuring, garment industry was separated from the spinning and weaving industries, early retirement of 18,000 workers is pursued, training and retraining programs are being introduced, technology upgrading, at a cost of LE 1.4 million is underway, a debt rescheduling arrangement is being worked out.

Syria

The overall picture

The Syrian economy is dominated by the primary sector with most activities generated by agriculture and hydrocarbon extraction. Most production is destined for domestic consumption. Exports are largely confined to oil. Industry, especially that considered strategic as textiles, food processing, chemicals, and domestic appliances, are firmly controlled by government through the state enterprise sector. The Syrian private sector is fragile though growing in scope and significance (Syria Report, 2002).

Externally oriented economic strategy (Lo or Hi)

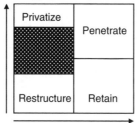

Enterprise competitive performance (Lo or Hi)

Figure 4.3   The strategic choice for Egypt's textile industry

The Syrian economy is going through a process of transformation. Measures taken in the past two years include protecting private assets from nationalization, granting specific privileges to private investors, allowing private banks, liberalizing foreign currency ownership and trading practices, and allowing private sector (including foreign) management of loss-making state enterprises. Big gaps remain, however. These relate to the legal infrastructure, the institutional framework, as well as the managerial practice.

Nevertheless, Syria enjoys a relatively relaxed position with regards to the speed and urge for adjustment. Syria was not forced to reschedule its debt via the international financial institutions and can afford to adopt policies within a controlled time framework that maintain a guiding role for the state and avoid the severe measures that are, by now, familiar in many other countries.

External orientation of the Syrian economy

The following table (Table 4.2) provides a measure of the external orientation parameters that we have referred to earlier. We can observe that the attributes of almost every parameter are way below the "benchmarks" that one could come across in a genuinely externally oriented economy as, say, that of Saudi Arabia in the Middle East or Thailand in the Far East. Contribution of exports to GDP, in Syria, stands at 34 percent (2004), FDI or Foreign Direct Investment is marginal and competitiveness is at a record low level.

Table 4.2   External orientation parameters of Syria

External orientation	Syria	
	2003	**2004**
Export of goods and services	31	34
Imports of goods and services	29	32
Foreign Direct Investment net	180	275
Competitiveness rank	(a) Global: n.a.	(a) Global: 104
	(b) Among Arab	(b) Among Arab
Foreign currency regime	Managed currency float	

Source: World Bank Fact Sheets 2004, 2005. World Economic Forum, Global Competitiveness Report, 2006

Competitiveness of Public Enterprise in Syria

Case of the Syrian Telecommunications Establishment (STE)

Syrian Public enterprise competitive performance does vary across industries. "Contemporary" sectors such as telecommunication and energy seem to be performing well, by national and maybe even regional standards. Others especially those in "traditional" industries such as textiles and food are haunted with a variety of problems that range from mediocre product quality and little market orientation to poor management and low productivity. Lack of investment funds and need for capacity modernization and upgrading seem to be common across all sectors.

The Syrian telecom industry, for example, is dominated by a major state operator, the Syrian Telecommunications Establishment (STE), a public sector body linked to the Ministry of Communications. The STE led the process of telecommunication network modernization in the 1990s (digitalization, fiber optic cables for inter-city transmissions, etc), and continues to expand Syria's telecommunication capacity. Closely associated with STE is the Syrian Korean Company, (SKC), a joint venture between the STE (51 percent) and Samsung (49 percent). The SKC manufactures telecommunication equipment.

Generally, Syria's telecommunications industry has performed well over the past few years. This could not be said, however, of other sectors such as banking and energy.

Emerging strategic choices

Syria's public enterprises seem to be more in need of restructuring than outright privatization (Figure 4.4). It all depends on the sector. Banking

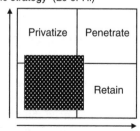

Externally oriented economic strategy (Lo or Hi)

| Privatize | Penetrate |
| Retain |

Enterprise competitive performance (Lo or Hi)

Figure 4.4   Syria's telecommunications position within the strategic options matrix

can do with both. Energy may require more privatization than restructuring. Telecommunication could do with partial privatization.

Saudi Arabia

The broad picture

Saudi Arabia has been embarking for years on a process of economic reform. The kingdom is promoting market freedom through privatization, creation of regulatory reform authorities, improving foreign investment laws, revising a broad range of business laws, and observing intellectual property rights. The kingdom is also becoming a more significant player in international trade by seeking membership in the World Trade Organization (WTO).

Privatization has become a priority in Saudi Arabia. It is driven by a desire to ease the government's public debt burden as well as the forecast future capital expenditure needs in vital sectors such as petrochemicals, electricity, water, telecommunications, gas, and information technology. These areas will require, over the next 20 years, an estimated US$800 billion investment. Steps are being taken towards privatizing several state entities including state hospitals, the postal services, the telephone system in order to build the capital base of this expenditure. Among the first to be privatized was the Saudi Telecommunications Co (STC), the kingdom's sole telecomm provider, whose shares went to private Saudi investors (20 percent) and the state pension funds (10 percent).

Altogether twenty vital economic sectors have been earmarked for privatization in Saudi Arabia. The kingdom's basic privatization objectives are clear: increasing employment opportunities, providing services to citizens and investors in a timely and cost efficient manner, rationalizing public expenditure, and reducing the burden on the government budget, as well as increasing government returns from the sale of assets.

External orientation of Saudi economy

An objective measure of Saudi Arabia's external orientation could be judged by reviewing the attributes of each of the variables referred to in the following table (Table 4.3). The conclusion is that the Saudi economy is going through an advanced stage of external orientation. Exports contribute, to nobody's surprise, 53 percent to the GDP with oil and gas as the prime movers. Foreign direct investment inflow is modest by many standards but the availability of a strong domestic capital base

Table 4.3 Saudi Arabia's external orientation parameters

External orientation	Saudi Arabia	
	2003	2004
Export of goods and services	46	53
Imports of goods and services	24	25
Foreign Direct Investment	0.78	1.94
Competitiveness rank	Among Arab countries: n.a.	Among Arab countries in 2005: 7
Foreign currency regime	Managed currency float	

Source: World Bank Fact Sheets 2004, 2005. World Economic Forum, Global Competitiveness Report, 2006

does explain that. Competitiveness rank, among Arab countries, was put at 7 by the World Economic Forum.

It is worth referring here to an IFC evaluation of the environment of commercial transactions in 155 countries and the rank that Saudi Arabia managed to achieve there. The report ranked countries according to a set of criteria that included business processes: starting a business, dealing with licenses, hiring and firing, registering property, getting credit, protecting investors, paying taxes, trading across borders, enforcing contracts, and closing a business. Saudi Arabia was ranked first among Arab countries followed by Kuwait.

Competitiveness of Public Enterprises in Saudi Arabia

Case of SABIC, Saudi Basic Industries Corporation

SABIC is, it goes without saying, a flagship for the Saudi public enterprise sector and could be viewed as a showcase as well. It relied, from the beginning on the following specific strategies for growth and global competitiveness:

1. diversifying the product portfolio;
2. establishing more joint ventures with industry majors;
3. placing greater emphasis on research and development;
4. diversifying further downstream.

Product diversification is prime among these strategies, a move triggered by the increased demand for methanol, ethylene, polyethylene, and ethylene in Saudi Arabia, and the mounting pressure on petrochemical producers to consider new products. These strategic moves fit within the Saudi government's overall policy of structural and institutional reform, and the desire for a sustained increase in private investment, including FDI, to help diversify the national economy and create job opportunities.

Competitiveness of Saudi public enterprises varied according to sector and positioning. A case in point is SABIC. Saudi Basic Industries Corporation is a public company: 70 percent of its shares are owned by the government of Saudi Arabia, and the other 30 percent by private shareholders in the kingdom and other Gulf Cooperation Council (GCC) states. It is one of the most competitive enterprises in Saudi Arabia in terms of profitability and market reach. And it is competitive internationally by many measures including geographical reach (presence in more than 100 countries), being one of the world's top 10 largest petrochemical companies, and the third in polyethylene production as well as fourth in polypropylene production. SABIC is also the world's single largest producer and exporter of granular urea fertilizer. "Within SABIC we are engaged in a process of redefining our businesses and our business strategies. Within Saudi Arabia, we are helping to build new learning and caring communities. Externally, we are inventing new markets with new alliances and partnerships" (World Economic Forum, interview with Mohamed Al-Mady, CEO, SABIC, 2006).

Emerging strategic choices

Saudi public enterprises operate within an open economy and demonstrate a high measure of competitiveness (Figure 4.5). Both conditions

Externally oriented economic strategy (Lo or Hi)

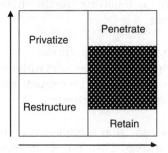

Figure 4.5   Saudi Arabia's SABIC's position with the strategy matrix

militate against a privatization strategy. The case of SABIC supports this notion. SABIC fits within Saudi Arabia's broad picture of an open economy and a significant global producer of commodity petrochemicals. This is a position that will only develop further in the course of the next decade with or without a privatization strategy.

Summary and conclusions

Privatization is a prevalent strategy made popular by the advent of free-market thinking. It is done in the name of efficiency, fiscal reward, wealth distribution, and competitiveness. Arab countries were, however, mild in their endorsement of this privatization strategy. The privatization efforts that began in Egypt in the late eighties, in Tunisia in the early nineties, and in Algeria in the late nineties, were, in reality, hesitant and, at times, shy. The scale was limited and the result was modest.

It is the author's contention that privatization is one of several strategies open to an economy or a country. Determinants of those strategies are two: the macro-economic policies pursued by the state and the competitive drive of the state enterprise or the industrial sector in question. Externally oriented macro-economic policies require the high degree of private ownership that privatization delivers. Low relative performance of state-owned enterprises, or enterprise sectors, creates a desire for better performance and the search for ways and means of achieving that.

Three countries and three state-owned enterprises were selected to test this hypothesis. Egypt was found to progress towards an externally oriented economy and to harbor ill performing, competitively weak state-owned enterprises in general and the spinning and weaving sector in particular. The conclusion was that privatization as a strategy is opportune but a restructuring strategy should precede it. Syria's external orientation was found to be lacking but this contrasted with a competitive and well-performing state-owned enterprise in the telecommunications sector. Our conclusion here was that Syria's public enterprises in the telecommunications sector are more in need of restructuring than outright privatization. As to Saudi Arabia, the situation there was probably the most advanced with regards to the external orientation of the economy and the competitive profile of the case enterprise, SABEC. The conclusion was against the perusal of a privatization strategy in this case.

Part II

Entrepreneurship

Introduction to Part II

Entrepreneurial initiative belongs to the heart of strategic behavior; Part II of this book attends to this notion.

It deals with entrepreneurship as a concept and as an application within an Arab context. The starting point is a broad identification of the main contours of the concept and what it came to represent over time. Classic works dealing with the personality of the entrepreneur and the drivers of business entrepreneurship provide the fundamental inputs.

This second chapter addresses the issue of personality and how the personality dimension of an Arab entrepreneur differs or is congruent with those identified elsewhere.

The third chapter addresses a key constraint, i.e. capital and finance. Attention is paid to venture capital and the availability or non-availability of that within the Middle East. It also deals with successful experiences of venture capital in an economy that did not have the experience before, e.g. the People's Republic of China. Islamic finance and the possible role of that as a boost to investment are also included in the analysis.

The final chapter handles the issue of strategy and does that along two lines. First is the role and function of family firms in Arab countries. Focus is placed on the Gulf States given the profound role of family business there. Analysis further attends to the issue of exit or termination of business and how a strategic decision like that functions within an Arab environment.

5
Conceptual and Operational Framework for Entrepreneurship

What is entrepreneurship?

Entrepreneurship is the process of identifying opportunities and exploiting those. Several scholars played a role in conceiving the concept and giving it its intellectual content; four did that with a distinction. They are Joseph Schumpeter, Peter Drucker, David McClleland, and Henry Mintzberg.

The understanding of entrepreneurship owes a lot to the work of Joseph Schumpeter and the Austrian School of economics. For Schumpeter (Schumpeter, 1950), an entrepreneur is a person who is willing and able to convert a new idea or invention into a successful business. Entrepreneurship forces "creative destruction" across markets and industries, simultaneously creating new products and business models, and killing others (Schumpeter, 1984). This so-called creative destruction is largely responsible for the dynamism of capitalism and the long-term economic growth associated with it.

Schumpeter placed the entrepreneur at the heart of the capitalist economic system to the extent that the eventual disappearance of the concept would lead to a collapse of the system itself. Fundamental to Schumpeter is innovation, meaning new products, new methods of production, new markets, new sources of raw material, new markets, and or new organizations.

Ducker's (1970) entrepreneurship is part and parcel of the workings of an economy and society. He underlines the risk taking, but he also pierces through to the future and paints a picture of the role of entrepreneurship in the years to come. Ducker states:

> what we need is an entrepreneurial society in which innovation and entrepreneurship are normal, steady and continual. Just as management

has become the specific a organ of all contemporary institutions, and the integrating organ of our society of organizations, so innovation and entrepreneurship have to become an integral life sustaining activity in our organizations, our economy, our society. (Ducker, 2001)

David McClelland is most noted for describing three types of motivational need (McClelland, 1961). These needs are found, to varying degrees, in all individuals within an organization and this mix characterizes a person's style and behavior, both in terms of being motivated, and in terms of managing and motivating others. Was McClelland's a measure of the desire to achieve? His n-ach (need for achievement) person is "achievement motivated" and therefore seeks achievement, attainment of realistic but challenging goals, and advancement in the job. There is a strong need for feedback as to achievement and progress, and a need for a sense of accomplishment.

Henry Mintzberg's contribution related to the managerial role of the entrepreneur and how different that is from "classic" managerial roles within organizations.

There are also others who made a contribution. These include Pinchot (1985) who coined the term "intrapreneurship" to describe entrepreneurial-like activities inside large business organizations as well as government. The concept is commonly referred to as corporate entrepreneurship. Wilken related the concept to environmental forces and the existence of a set of cultural, economic, political, and economic forces (Wilken, 1979). And, more recently, Ketz de Vries explored the "dark" side of the entrepreneurial personality and the impact that has on role fulfillment.

Entrepreneurship is widely regarded as an integral player in the business culture of American life, particularly as an engine for job creation and economic growth (Sobel, 1974).

Who is an entrepreneur?

Views vary and range from the rational to the romantic! Entrepreneurs are described sometimes as heroes, sometimes as invisible forces and yet some other times as ordinary men and women. Most commonly, the term entrepreneur applies to someone who establishes a new entity to offer a new or existing product or service into a new or existing market. Joseph Schumpeter, resorting to the norms of the culture of his era, was probably the first to call the entrepreneur a hero. He placed him at the center of the economic system, considering him the most dynamic engine of growth within the capitalist system. In the intellectual construction of the Austrian economist, the entrepreneur was so central that when the role was taken over by a large structured organization, some of the premises of the capitalist system were challenged.

Viewed in more contemporary terms, entrepreneurs are looked at as agents of change and prophets of innovation. These views have been expressed by several authors in the light of contemporary studies of people who demonstrated entrepreneurial initiative. Modern day entrepreneurs confirm this profile. Recognized American entrepreneurs such as John D. Rockefeller (Oil), Henry Ford (automobiles), J. Pierpont Morgan (banking), Thomas Edison (electricity/light bulbs), George Eastman (cameras), Milton S. Hershey (candy) contributed to the aura and the myth.

Contemporary concepts also introduce the element of vision and "thrill" into entrepreneurship. There are those who describe entrepreneurs as individuals who are able to conceive a vision and generate a "thrill" Both are reflections of a strong belief in a concept or an opportunity and the willingness to accept a high level of personal, professional, or financial risk to pursue that opportunity. Entrepreneurial vision entails a mental perception of the kind of environment an individual or an organization aspires to create within a broad time horizon and the underlying conditions for the actualization of this perception. It is a description of something (an organization, a corporate culture, a business, a technology, an activity) in the future. It could also be a "concept of a new and desirable future reality that can be communicated throughout the organization." Entrepreneurs perceive their visions and do not ask themselves whether they have one. Having a vision implies involvement, commitment, and total immersion. All efforts stem from it and all forces and structures are seen in terms of their relevance to its existence. Issues such as rest and reward become secondary as attention is focused on the prime target, i.e. vision fulfillment (Drucker, 1970).

What do entrepreneurs do?

Entrepreneurs perform two prime functions: actualization and management. Actualization refers to the conversion of vision into a business venture. Management refers to the actual running of the organization that has been created. Each process is independent and implies different things.

Actualization involves:

- Translation of vision into concrete business processes;
- Capitalization and fund mobility;
- Human resource identification, assignment, and coordination;
- Sourcing of production or service inputs;
- Market approach;
- Product and service delivery;
- Strategic thinking of the next phases of the venture.

As to the managerial role, Mintzberg's classical analysis of the managerial roles of the entrepreneur (Mintzberg, 1973) provides a comprehensive framework. More recent analysis confirms the picture and supports the findings. Table 5.1 depicts those different managerial roles and the time assigned to them in Mintzberg's test.

Interpersonal roles

- Acts as figurehead of the company performing a variety of public, but routine duties of a legal or social nature.
- Provides leadership by performing activities involving directing, coordinating, and controlling.
- Maintains a network of outside contacts that provide favors and information.

Informational roles

- Gathers information, detects changes, identifies potential opportunities and problems, builds up knowledge, and is informed of important information that must be disseminated within the company.
- Disseminates information within the company by sending external information into the organization and deciding on distributing internal information to appropriate subordinates.
- Transmits information to outsiders on company plans, polices, actions, and results.

Decisional roles

- Searches the environment for new opportunities and initiates projects to bring about change.
- Decides corrective actions needed when the company faces important, often unexpected internal problems.
- Decides the allocation of resources in the company.
- Represents the company in major negotiations with outsiders.

Table 5.1 The impact of Mintzberg identified entrepreneurial roles on decision making

Behavior and response to managerial role (1)	Mean	Importance to managerial role	
		Unimportant	Important
Entrepreneur	5.49	8.4	91.6
Liaison	5.38	11.9	88.1
Monitor	5.21	16.6	83.4
Spokesman	5.07	21.9	78.1
Negotiator	4.87	24.6	75.4
Disturbance handler	4.78	23.7	76.3
Resource allocator	4.69	27.5	72.5
Leader	4.53	33.5	66.5
Figure head	4.28	37.1	62.9
Disseminator	4.26	32.0	68.0

(1) The managerial roles are those identified by Mintzberg. (1973)
(2) Unimportant defined by ratings of 1–3 and important defined by ratings of 4–7.
Source: Mintzberg (1973)

What do entrepreneurs possess?

Entrepreneurial traits?

There is myth and there is reality here. Myth does, at times, exceed reality. North American literature projects a "hero" image of the entrepreneur and views him as the warrior who enters and conquers. A more mundane picture developed within and outside the United States, would provide an inventory of what one may consider "realistic" traits and an equal list of "observed" traits. To the realistic views belong the following:

• A desire to achieve. This is the inner force that creates the desire to seek challenge and the drive to fulfill that challenge. It is the insistence coming from within to be recognized for a business success. The ever burning desire to set goals and see them fulfilled.

• An eye for opportunities. Entrepreneurs look at the world through different eyes. They presume to posses the far sight and the vision that would unmask a business opportunity and define its contours. This is what differentiates an entrepreneur from an ordinary person. It is that sense of a business possibility.

• A measure of risk taking. Entrepreneurs are risk takers. They are able to develop a reasonable sense of the size and the magnitude of risk involved in actualizing an opportunity. They balance risks and gains and weigh them both. So entrepreneurs take risks, but they are usually calculated risks.

- A bias for action. After conceiving of an idea, calculating the risks versus the benefits, and making strategic decisions, the entrepreneur take the initiative by turning those intentions into realities. They do not allow the vastness of an endeavor to grip them with fear.
- Creativity and innovation. Entrepreneur's identification of opportunities is associated, in many cases, with a sense of creation and innovation. Whether it is a new technology or a new way of solving an old problem, entrepreneurs have been considered the people who were on the cutting edge of many industries.

These are traditional traits; they are usually associated with a set of other traits that include:

- Passion. Most successful entrepreneurs view their work in terms of it being a mission. They not only love their work but regard it with dedication and zeal.
- Hard work. A strong work ethic is the engine that powers small business' success.
- Competitiveness. Most successful entrepreneurs don't like to lose and when they do fail, they aren't afraid to get back out there and try again. They are willing to test their abilities against those of others and even thrive on the competition.
- Perseverance. The ability to keep goals in sight and maintain a sense of perspective when facing the myriad of problems and obstacles that meet entrepreneurs is essential.
- Adaptability. Entrepreneurs have the ability to find creative solutions for a variety of situations and problems. This ability to step outside the box or think outside the box is not easy and may require some unorthodox approaches.
- Ability to organize. Undertaking a venture requires both discipline and structure. Structuring of processes that should take place and defining the right priorities. And a discipline to see them through.
- Perseverance. Entrepreneurs must deal with many types of people when doing business. They have to talk to lawyers, accountants, bankers, employees, and customers. They must be able to get people interested in their business ideas and persuade them to help attain their goals.
- Optimism. Entrepreneurs see obstacles and challenges as opportunities. Their outlook on life is positive. The glass is half full.

To summarize, entrepreneurs are, generally, hard-working, driven, emotionally charged, overly energetic individuals, who will judge both themselves and their environment in challenging terms. They strive to maintain absolute control over their destinies. They are goal-oriented and have low tolerance for failure. They have large egos needing to be nurtured. They tend to believe they are always right, and it is difficult for them to accept advice or heed council. They are calculated risk takers.

They are good communicators who can generate enthusiasm within others because they believe so deeply in their cause. They are, generally, weak in money matters, seeing cash only as a means to an end, rather than as an essential commodity needing to be constantly and carefully monitored. Either they are so positive they will succeed that financial planning seems irrelevant to them, or they are so uncomfortable in dealing with finances that they avoid money matters as much as possible.

Above all, they are visionaries. They see a vision of the future, and they strive against all odds to make their vision a reality.

The roots of entrepreneurial behavior

Capitalist free market systems

Capitalist thinking carries the roots of entrepreneurial behavior. As we will argue hereafter, capitalist thinking is essentially a system with inputs, outputs, and a transformation mechanism; entrepreneurial initiative lies at the heart of each element of this system (Figure 5.1).

Put very simply and at considerable cost in rigor, capitalist thinking could be viewed as a system with inputs and outputs, a transformation mechanism and a feedback loop. General systems theory lends itself perfectly to this kind of analysis. It provides a framework for understanding and integrating knowledge from a wide variety of highly specialized fields (Boulding, 1956). It also allows for system differentiation and system dynamics. There are open systems and closed systems. There are functional systems and cross-functional systems. What matters within the context of this analysis is that the general systems theory gives us a powerful tool to examine, analyzes, and explore the dynamics of capitalism and the inner processes of the ideology.

Inputs

In the capitalist system these are built around three prime components: Premises, Players and Resources. Premises are system building blocks or

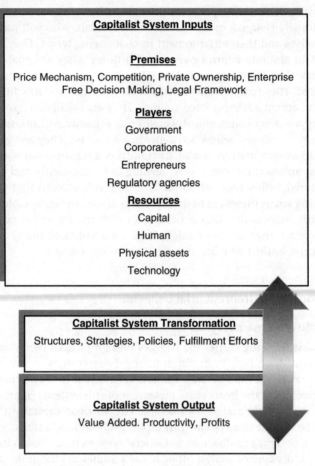

Figure 5.1　The building blocks of the capitalist system

elements that constitute the texture of the body of the system. Players are actors performing certain roles that are dictated by system dynamics. Resources are energy components essential for system operations. While premises provide the foundation and the framework, actors exploit the resources in order to produce the ultimate output.

Premises of capitalist economic structure include:

- Markets;
- A price mechanism;
- Competition;

- Private ownership;
- Enterprise spirit;
- Free decision making;
- A legal framework.

Markets are the arenas where the demand and supply forces interact in order to produce a transaction. The price mechanism is the medium through which market forces express themselves. Competition is a measure of rivalry pertinent to market behavior. Private ownership is the expression of a right that allows effective market performance. Enterprise spirit is the trigger of the dynamic all-inclusive interactive processes of the market. Free decision-making is the unconstrained search for opportunities and fulfillment. And the legal framework is the boundary that separates right from wrong (transaction).

The fundamental insight here is that the major price and resource allocation decisions are made in markets (Samuelson, 1995).

Players

In the capitalist system, these are actors performing functions essential for the ultimate fulfillment of capitalist ideology. The executive branch, or government, is a player. But so are also the corporations, the entrepreneurs, and the wide variety of functional, task-focused institutions operating within the capitalist arena:

- Governments play the role of a guardian and a caretaker. They guard system efficiency (resource allocation), preserve system equity (income distribution), stimulate growth (monetary and fiscal policies), and provide essential public goods. They also provide the legal framework essential for a proper flow of events.
- Corporations assume the task of exploiting market opportunities and, in the process, creating value added, fulfilling consumer demand, and generating employment. Good corporations have visionary management, are responsive to market conditions, and are driven by technological change.
- Entrepreneurs are a key player within the capitalist arena. Their prime role is that of opportunity identification and opportunity conversion into a tangible business venture. The entrepreneur is both an opportunity seeker and a risk taker. He or she is self-motivated, has a keen desire to achieve, and maintains an inner locus for control, and possesses, in many cases, a vision that guides acts and deeds.

• Institutions are structures created to draw a framework for functional and sectorial performance. They could assume a regulatory function. Their roots can lie in the corporate sector, the enterprise class, or even government.

Resources, in the capitalist system are those factors of production contributing directly to the process of production and dissemination of goods and services. These include:

• Capital is a production factor that is built around a physical and/or a monetary base. The physical base takes the form of factories, equipment, and inventories. The financial base takes the form of money, stocks, and bonds;
• Human resources;
• Physical resources.

Transformation mechanism

The capitalist version is a blend of policies, strategies, and fulfillment efforts exercised in search of value added. Prime among these are policies, more specifically macro economic policies. To these belong:

• Trade policies;
• Industrial policies;
• Monetary policies;
• Fiscal policies;
• Wage policies;
• Investment policies;
• Price policies;
• Employment policies.

The output

This is probably the most obvious component of the system as it connotes value added, productivity, and, ultimately, profits.

Three breeds of capitalism

Capitalist thinking is far from uniform. There are varieties: the Anglo-Saxon variety, the European variety, and the Asian variety. Differences between the three varieties could be wide. One area, for example, is that of labor and labor costs. The Anglo-Saxon model strives for lower labor coasts, the European model makes that a function of productivity and competition, while the Asian model relates labor cost to competition. Yet another area is financial markets. These are regarded in the Anglo-Saxon model as supreme, while the European and Asian models regard them as supportive and an integral part of the system. A third area is competition which is regarded in the Anglo-Saxon model as optimum while it is associated with a certain measure of inequality in Europe and the culture in Asia (Albert, 1993).

What really distinguishes the Anglo-Saxon breed of capitalism is its inherent uncertainty about the present and pessimism about the future. At the heart of these symptoms lies assumption that capitalisms in general and American capitalism in particular are systems where power works well on its own terms, when the power of the capitalist class is secure and not too costly to maintain. When that "power. is under-mined – either by groups or by the contradictory nature of capitalist's own objectives or when it becomes very costly to maintain, the capitalist economy is likely to falter" (Bowles and Edwards, 1993).

Implications of capitalist and free market thinking for entrepreneurship

Entrepreneurship's deep roots into capitalist and free market thinking have direct impact on two key issues: choice or work and innovation.

One of the most important implications of capitalist thinking is the choice given to each and every individual between paid work and entre-preneurial initiative. This choice is most explicit in the United States, especially if one is to compare the level of choice there to that in Europe or several other parts of the world. Recent EU research revealed a higher preference for entrepreneurial initiative in the United States than that in Europe (See Table 5.2 below). A near 59 percent of American respon-dents to the survey preferred self-employment compared to 47 percent in Europe (2003 data). European data demonstrated a measure of stabil-ity over time too. The figures for 2001 and 2002 do not deviate that much from those of 2003 (EU, 2004).

Yet another implication is the fundamental one that innovation in general and entrepreneurship-related innovation in particular is taking in contemporary capitalist thinking. This is expressed by Drucker when he states: "Innovation and entrepreneurship are ... needed in society as much as in the economy, in public service institutions as much as in business". Also the fact the innovation is bound to start within the

Table 5.2   Preference for self employment in the United States and the EU (2001–2003)

Category	European Union		United States	
	2002	2003	2002	2003
Would rather be an employee	50	49	29	35
Would rather be an employer	45	47	67	59

Source: Gallop Europe, 2004

Table 5.3   The shifting value system

Money and Capital	Yesterday's ideas	Today's principles
Source	Work Business productivity	Investment Own productivity/ through own business
Creating Cumulating	Household assets Knowledge	Managing own net worth Creating Personal Strategic Competitive Advantage (PSCA) Creating a Market Portfolio
Controlling	Market dependent	Potential dependent

boundaries of small business. "Innovation had better be capable of being started small, requiring at first little money, few people and only a small and limited market. Otherwise there is not enough time to make the adjustments and changes that are almost always needed for an innovation to succeed" (Drucker, 2001). He also adds [m]core competencies are different for every organization, they are, so to speak, part of an organization's personality. But every organization – not just businesses – needs one core competence: innovation".

And finally, one has to stress the overall change in societal norms and values and the general shift away from the concept of "paid employment" to the concept of "created value added." This notion is represented in Table 5.3, where the contrast between the paid employment phenomenon and wealth creation and value added generation concept is illustrated.

How to measure entrepreneurship

There are two routes to measurement: the Propensity to Enterprise measure and the Entrepreneurial Activity measure. The first was developed by the author as an aggregate measure of entrepreneurial practice within an economy. The second goes a step further and makes a distinction between different types of entrepreneurial initiative and the different points of time where an entrepreneurial intent is declared and an entrepreneurial act is consummated.

The "propensity to enterprise" or the relationship between self-employment and total employment within an economy (El Namaki, 1996). I have relied on the standards created by ILO for defining both self-employment and total employment. Self-employment was related to employers as well as own-account workers. An employer is a "person who operates his or her own economic enterprise or engages independently in a profession or trade, and hires one or more employees." An own-account worker is a "person who operates his or her own economic enterprise or engages independently in a profession or trade and hires no employees." The economically active population is defined as "all persons of either sex who furnish the supply of labor for the production of economic goods and services as defined by the United Nations systems of national accounts and balances, during a specified time-reference period" (ILO, 2004) (Table 5.4).

Another approach to the measurement of entrepreneurship is that adopted by GEM (GEM, 2004). GEM measures TEA or Total Entrepreneurial

Table 5.4 Comparative propensity to enterprise ratios for a number of emerging economies

Comparative PTE in a few emerging economies	Year	Employers (million)	Own account workers (million)	Propensity to Enterprise (PTE)
Malaysia	1997	6.38	1.45	7.8
	2003	7.52	1.54	9.1
Thailand	1997	0.75	9.87	10.06
	2003	1.14	10.91	11.1
Taiwan	1997	0.50	1.52	2.02
	2002	0.50	1.50	2.00

Source: ILO Laborsta (Internet)/International Labor Statistics, 2004

Activity, a composite concept where several types of entrepreneurial initiatives are blended. Four types are distinguished:

1. Nascent entrepreneur. These are entrepreneurs actively planning a new venture. They have started a new venture within the past 12 months.
2. New firm entrepreneurs are those who either fully or partly own or manage a new business. The time dimension here is 4 to 42 months.
3. Early stage entrepreneurs are those who are going through the early stages of a business venture.
4. Established entrepreneur or individuals who have set up businesses.

Results of the GEM analysis could be summarized in the Table 5.5 below. Country selection is judgmental and is essentially determined by a country's readiness to participate in the survey. The table provides an overview of the different stages of entrepreneurial activity measured by GEM. The early stage prevalence rate or TEA index is the combined count of nascent entrepreneurs and new business owners, while the overall rate of entrepreneurial activity is the count of early stage plus established entrepreneurs. A small number of individuals qualify for more than one of the entrepreneurial stages because they are involved in more than one venture. The combined early stage index and the overall index count these individuals only once.

How to make entrepreneurs

There are different thoughts about this Entrepreneurship literature can be classified into two schools: one taking the supply-side perspective and the other, the demand-side perspective. The supply-side school

Table 5.5 Prevalence rates of entrepreneurial activities for selected countries according to GEM

Country	Nascent entrepreneurial activity	New business owners	Early stage entrepreneurial activity	Established business owners	Overall business owners	Number of observations
	As percentage of observations (%)					
Canada	6.6	3.6	9.3	7.4	16.6	5519
Japan	1.1	1.1	2.2	5.4	7.4	1931
Singapore	3.9	3.7	7.2	4.7	11.9	3876
China	5.6	9.4	13.7	13.2	26.7	2109

Source: GEM 2005

focuses on the availability of individuals with the right "traits" and characteristics to occupy entrepreneurial roles; the demand-side focuses on the forces that generate the entrepreneurial opportunity in the first place and, with it, the volume of entrepreneurial roles that need to be filled. The supply-side school examines entrepreneurship by focusing on the individual characteristics of entrepreneurs, specifying potential mechanisms for agency and change, whereas the demand-side emphasizes the push and pull of context.

Prime among the supply side schools are those focusing on the characteristics and the traits of the entrepreneur; classic among those is McClelland's motivational thinking school. To the same supply-side belongs the sociological school of thought with as a prime contributor. Finally demand-side was made evident by yet another classic work on entrepreneurship, i.e. that of Wilken who found that in historical perspective environmental conditions including the role of the state, played a major role in creation of an entrepreneurial class in selected countries in Western Europe.

The psychology school of thought is prominent in both literature and approach to entrepreneurial development and is worth further examination here.

The psychology school of thought was pioneered by David McClelland. He started workplace motivational thinking, developing achievement-based motivational theory and models. David McClelland is most noted for describing three types of motivational need (McClelland, 1961). These needs are found to varying degrees in all individuals within an organization and this mix of motivational needs characterizes a person's style and behavior, both in terms of being motivated, and of managing and motivating others:

- The need for achievement (n-ach). The n-ach person is "achievement motivated" and therefore seeks achievement, attainment of realistic but challenging goals, and advancement in the job. There is a strong need for feedback as to achievement and progress, and a need for a sense of accomplishment.
- The need for authority and power (n-pow). The n-pow person is "authority motivated." This driver produces a need to be influential, effective, to make an impact. There is a strong need to lead and for their ideas to prevail. There is also motivation and need towards increasing personal status and prestige.
- The need for affiliation (n-affil). The n-affil person is "affiliation motivated," has a need for friendly relationships, and is motivated

towards interaction with other people. The affiliation driver produces motivation, need to be liked and held in popular regard. These people are team players.

McClelland's particular fascination was for achievement motivation; his laboratory experiments illustrated that while most people do not possess a strong achievement-based motivation, those who do, display a consistent behavior in setting goals. Typically, achievement-motivated individuals set goals which they can influence with their effort and ability, and as such the goal is considered to be achievable. This determined results-driven approach is almost invariably present in the character make-up of all successful business people and entrepreneurs.

McClelland suggested other characteristics and attitudes of achievement-motivated people:

- Achievement is more important than material or financial reward.
- Achieving the aim or task gives greater personal satisfaction than receiving praise or recognition.
- Financial reward is regarded as a measurement of success, not an end in itself.
- Security is not prime motivator, nor is status.
- Feedback is essential, because it enables measurement of success, not for reasons of praise or recognition (the implication here is that feedback must be reliable, quantifiable, and factual).
- Achievement-motivated people constantly seek improvements and ways of doing things better.
- Achievement-motivated people will logically favor jobs and responsibilities that naturally satisfy their needs, i.e. offer flexibility and opportunity to set and achieve goals, e.g. sales and business management, and entrepreneurial roles.

McClelland firmly believed that achievement-motivated people are generally the ones who make things happen and get results, and that this extends to getting results through the organization of other people and resources, although as stated earlier, they often demand too much of their staff because they prioritize achieving the goal above the many varied interests and needs of their people.

Looking at the demand-side we may consider several authors who advance the notion that environmental factors stimulate the personality dimension and induce entrepreneurial action. A classic model is that of Wilken (1979) where he addresses the question whether industrial entrepreneurship is mainly the result of favorable economic conditions or whether socio-cultural and psychological factors affect the emergence of entrepreneurs and their performance beyond what might be expected from economic conditions alone. His conclusion argues for a blend of factors as the trigger of entrepreneurial initiative.

Kreuger and Brazeal suggest that beliefs, perceptions, and assumptions are learned within the context of a given environment (such as a business or community). They also argue that these attitudes and perceptions predict intentions which in turn influence behavior. Thus by indirect relationship, the Kreuger and Brazeal model suggests that the environment or event causes an individual to form perceptions, attitudes, and assumptions. These perceptions then translate themselves into intentions, or potential, which are expressed through behavior.

They conclude that, like the intention to act entrepreneurially, the decision to continue behavior is influenced by the interaction of various factors. These include individual characteristics, individual environment, business environment, an individual's personal goal set, and the existence of a viable business idea. Through these interacting factors, individuals make several comparisons between their perceptions of a probable outcome, their intended goals, intended behavior, and actual outcomes. The model predicts that when the outcomes meet or exceed perceived outcomes, positive behavior (continued engagement in entrepreneurialism) is reinforced. It also predicts that the opposite occurs when the perceived outcomes are not met. This model clearly incorporates psychological, behavioral, and situational factors.

Summary and conclusions

Entrepreneurship is the process of identifying opportunities and exploiting them.

Several scholars have contributed to origination of the concept and giving it its intellectual content, but four of those did that with distinction: Joseph Schumpeter, Peter Drucker, David McClelland, and Henry Mintzberg The understanding of entrepreneurship owes a lot to the work of Joseph Schumpeter and the Austrian School of economics. In Schumpeter (Schumpeter, 1950), an entrepreneur is a person who is willing and able to convert a new idea or invention into a successful business. Entrepreneurship forces "creative destruction" across markets and industries, simultaneously creating new products and business models and killing others. One of the most important implications of capitalist thinking is the choice given to each and every individual between paid work and entrepreneurial initiative.

Entrepreneurs perform two prime functions: actualization and management. Actualization refers to the conversion of personal vision into a business venture. Management refers to the actual running of the organization. Each process is independent and implies different things. There is myth and there is reality here. Myth does, at times, exceed reality. North American literature projects a "hero" image of the entrepreneur; the view is that of the warrior who enters and conquers. A more mundane picture developed within and outside the United States; it would provide an inventory of what one may consider "realistic" traits and an equal list of "observed."

Entrepreneurship literature can be classified into two schools, one taking the supply-side perspective and the other, the demand-side. The supply-side school focuses on the availability of individuals with the right "traits" and characteristics to occupy entrepreneurial roles; the demand side focuses on the forces that generate the entrepreneurial opportunity in the first place and, with it, the volume of entrepreneurial roles that need to be filled.

6
Personality of the Arab Entrepreneur

6.1 Entry, survival and death of the Arab entrepreneur

The problem

Small business is a powerful tool of economic growth. It generates employment, creates new businesses, adds value added, stimulates exports, substitutes imports and complements large business. This has proved to be the case in countries as varied as Thailand, Ireland, and Japan. In Thailand the small business sector provides the backbone of several critical industries (e.g. apparel, food, and electric appliances), is the non-replaceable working partner of the multinational corporations operating in critical sectors (automotives, information technology, food, etc), and is looked at as a significant player in the all too critical tourism sector. In Ireland, the small business sector was a powerful tool within the tool box of several Irish government agencies as the IDA (Irish Development Authority) during the early stages of economic growth; their innovative approach to private initiative stimulation and small enterprise survival provides a classic case. Japan relied, also, on the growth of small rural enterprises with policies crafted to produce effective linkages between smaller and larger firms. Today a near 74 percent of the country's industrial workforce is employed by small and medium size businesses.

Small business does not, unfortunately, play the same role and demonstrate the same dominance in most Arab countries. If we are to go by volumes, the number of small businesses per capita, does not compare to those in, for example, Thailand, Malaysia, Korea, or even Taiwan. The contribution of the sector to employment, new enterprise creation, exports, and even value added, is less than impressive. This despite government efforts and considerable and consistent expenditure on stimulated entry and protected existence. Why? There are four possible answers:

1. Pre-entry flaws;
2. Precarious existence of those who enter;
3. Lack of tools for survival;
4. Lack of knowledge about how to exit.

All of these are diseases or sicknesses that befall the small business and exert a price.

The following pages deal with this phenomenon. The point of start is an examination of the state of self-employment in those Arab countries for which data were available. This is followed by an analysis of the phenomenon of sickness of a small enterprise: the volumes, the symptoms, and the triggers. The final section deals with the remedies and recommendations with a focus on four areas: pre-entry guidance, post-entry survival, post entry turn around, and end-game strategies.

The terms small business, small enterprise, small firm, and self-employment are used interchangeably in this chapter.

This chapter is based on primary as well as secondary sources. The primary source covers a wide variety of small businesses and small business guidance agencies interviewed in Egypt, Syria, Jordan, and the United Arab Emirates. To the secondary source belong the writing and research of the staff of the World Bank, UNIDO, ILO, and several other international organizations; also research, albeit limited, done on the issue by several in the Arab countries themselves.

State of self-employment in selected Arab countries

Economies create jobs and small business and self-employment is the main engine. Arab countries are no exception.

To get a realistic picture of the state of the small business and self-employment in Arab countries, the author resorted to the International Labor Statistics of ILO (International Labor Organization). ILO is, probably, the only globally reliable source of data of this nature, and the source with a common base for a comparative analysis. The result of all of that was the following:

Self-employment

Table 6.1 shows the level of self-employment in those Arab countries for which data are available. Self-employment is viewed by the author as

Table 6.1 Self-employment (employers and own-account workers) in selected Arab countries and comparative data from South East Asia (1997–2003)

Arab countries	Year	Employers (in millions)	Own account workers (in millions)	Total employers and own account workers (in millions)
Egypt	1997	2.34	3.13	5.57
	2002	1.95	1.99	3.94
Morocco	2002	0.22	2.48	2.70
	2003	0.24	2.51	2.75
Palestine	1997	0.03	0.11	0.14
	2003	0.21	0.16	0.37
Yemen	1999	0.8	1.12	1.93
Syria	1997	n.a.	n.a.	n.a.
	2002	n.a.	n.a.	n.a.

Comparative PTE in a few emerging economies	Year	Employers (million)	Own account workers (million)	Propensity to Enterprise (PTE)
Malaysia	1997	6.38	1.45	7.8
	2003	7.52	1.54	9.1
Thailand	1997	0.75	9.87	10.06
	2003	1.14	10.91	11.1
Taiwan	1997	0.50	1.52	2.02
	2002	0.50	1.50	2.00

Source: ILO Laborsta (Internet)/International Labor Statistics, 2004. El Namaki (1996)

the grand total of two independent ILO categories: "Employers" and "Own Account Workers." Employers are defined by ILO as "... Persons who operate their own economic enterprise or engage independently in a profession or trade, and hire one or more employees." "Own Account Workers" are defined, again in the language of ILO, as person or persons who operate his or her own economic enterprise, or engages independently in a profession or trade. The grand total or sum of both should represent the total "reservoir" of independent employment, or small businesses, operating in a country.

Propensity to enterprise (PTE)

Table 6.2 introduces the concept of "Propensity to enterprise" (PTE) or, as we said in an earlier chapter, the relationship between self-employment

Table 6.2 The propensity to enterprise in selected Arab countries and the comparative level for Thailand and Malaysia (1997–2003)

Arab countries	Year	Total employers and own account workers (millions)	Total economically active population (millions)	Per capita enterprise level	Propensity to Enterprise (PTE) %
Egypt	1997	5.57	15.8		35
	2002	4.08	17.9	0.06	23
Morocco	2002	2.70	9.5		28
	2003	2.75	9.6	0.09	29
Palestine	1997	0.13	0.48		27
	2002	0.31	0.49		63
	2003	0.37	0.59		62
Yemen	1999	1.92	3.6		53
Syria	1997	n.a.	n.a		–
	2002	n.a.	n.a		–
Comparative case countries					
Taiwan	1997	2.02	9.2		22
	2002	2.00	9.4		21
Thailand	1997	10.6	33.2		32
	2002	10.7	34.3	0.18	29
	2003	11.1	34.7		32

Source: ILO Laborstat (internet)/International Labor Statistics 2004. El Namaki (1996)

and the total volume of economically active population within an economy (El Namaki, 1996). It is expressed as the percentage of those within the economically active segment of the population who opt for self-employment (and small enterprise) as an economic venue. Economically active populations are defined, again according to the ILO as "all persons of either sex who furnish the supply of labor for the production of economic goods and services as defined by the United Nations systems of national accounts and balances, during a specified time-reference period." PTE, is a proxy measure of the entrepreneurial initiative and the drive towards independent business initiative in a country or an economy.

Positive change in the ratio over time is a reflection of a greater penetration of forces of the free market and the underlying principles of enterprise. It could also be a response to stimulatory measures taken by the government within economic policy adjustment programs, or even an economic ideology shift. It could also, finally, embody a reshaping of the cultural forces underlying the behavior of individuals within a community. We have to add that it could also be a reflection of the lack of other viable economic alternatives.

The PTE seems also to be negatively associated with economic growth. Put differently, economic growth leads, as data reveal, to greater dependence on paid employment. The explanation could be the change in the structure of an economy as it grows, and the greater reliance on large corporations to provide value added. It could also relate to the impact of the external orientation of the economy and the reliance on foreign goods and services that are more competitive than local ones.

An observation that could strike the reader of Table 6.1 is the visible absence of data for key Arab countries such as Syria, Saudi Arabia, and Yemen. The data may be elsewhere, but they are not available within an international context such as ILO. And for an economically significant and politically sensitive sector as small business in a country like Syria, this is a serious omission.

It is my opinion that a Propensity to Enterprise should be in the range of 16–40 percent for developing and emerging economies and 15 percent or less for developed and maturing economies (El Namaki, 1996). Indonesia and the Philippines, for example, had, in 1990, a PTE of 42.4 percent and 35.2 percent respectively, while the United States and Japan scored 8.2 percent and 12.7 percent in the same year. A possible explanation is in the argument that emerging economies generate more growth opportunities for those who are seeking entrepreneurial initiative than developed economies. Also that the labor market of emerging economies is usually structured in a way that paid employment is not the major source of jobs and occupations. Finally, the fact that global industry concentration usually works against a developing country's employment.

Figures emerging for Egypt and Morocco (23 percent and 29 percent in 2002 respectively), are congruent with the international norm. The problem, however, is in the trend and the absolute numbers. As to the trend, it is downward in the case of Egypt and nearly constant in the case of Morocco, and that is a bad omen. As to the *per capita* level, a gap is there. Thailand's *per capita* enterprise level stands at 0.18 (almost two persons out of ten are self- employed) which is considerably higher than that of Egypt. The comparison with Thailand is relevant here given the proximity of conditions to those in many Arab countries, especially Egypt.

Small business sickness in Arab countries

Business creation is one side of the story; business failure and termination are the other side. As data on Arab countries are nearly non-existent, and we have to depend on judgmental views complemented by some of the common international standards developed over the years.

Most bankruptcies in an economy occur in smaller and younger firms. The management of a new firm faces a learning curve. In the early stages of the firm's life, internal deficiencies are so prevalent that most bankruptcies occur for these reasons. The source is most likely management's failure at mastering the basic internal skills of general management, finance, marketing, control, communications, supervision, and market development (Figure 6.1).

As the surviving firm grows, a new set of problems arise that are associated with the increased complexity of running an older and often larger firm. Managerial issues such as unwillingness to delegate responsibilities, departure of key personnel, succession, division of work, allocation of rewards, and motivation of personnel, all lead to a second cycle of enterprise failure.

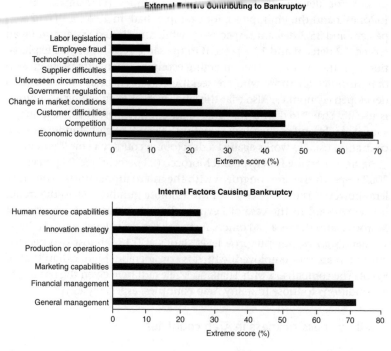

Figure 6.1 External and internal factors contributing to bankruptcy of small business in Canada

Table 6.3 Estimated rates of small business failure across countries (1990s data)

Stage	Time frame	An estimation of rates of failure (as percentage of the starting numbers)
Entry	First year	Up to 70%
Survival	Up to ten years	A maximum of 30%
Growth	Up to ten years from inception	Less than 10%

Source: Several sources including *USA Today* (for American small firms), *Financial Times* (for UK small firms), WB Research (for Taiwan enterprises)

It may be worth stressing here that the death of a small firm may not be terminal. In the USA, a 1994 survey of those who had failed in business revealed that, more than 53% became owners of another business. When asked if they would have done it all over again, 61.4% said "Yes."

Sources of sickness

Earlier work by the author suggests that there are different types of barriers that constrain small business creation and growth. There are entry barriers, survival barriers, and exit barriers. Such barriers are universal, and they apply to individuals as well as the sector as a whole. Table 6.3 is an analysis of those barriers (El Namaki, 1988, 1989):

Entry barriers

Motivation

Becoming an entrepreneur is largely a psychological and sociological process. This process rests on a base of motivation, forward thinking, and vision (El Namaki, 1992). These elements either exist within the individual, the commercial environment, or they are generated by external forces. Facilitating an intermediary agencies usually do that. An attempt is being made at that in Dubai, through the work of specialized foundations as well as government economic development agencies, but the road is long.

Regulation

Small business is regulated, in Egypt for example, by approximately 18 different laws and 22 ministries and government institutions. An attempt at entry is akin to a jump in the dark. The demands are often contradictory and verge on the absurd (department of antiquities has to sanction a request for a retail outlet, for example!).

Minority status

This applies, primarily, to women although it could apply to other ethnic groups who are not given sufficient recognition. The issue of women is controversial given the claims often made that women are given equal rights and their ability to start or operate a business is far from restricted. It remains true, however, that women in Arab countries face networking, visibility, finance, and contracting constraints that undermine their ability to participate, fully, in the business process.

Lack of identity

Definitions of small business vary and there are times when no-one really knows what a small business is. Most laws and regulations adhere to an amorphous silhouette of what could eventually constitute a small business. This problem of identify creates consequent problems in assistance granting, support, and even exit.

Non-guided project choice

Identification of a venture could result from a myriad of factors and assistance is needed to assess the alternatives with highest probability of success. Economic growth in the UAE is leading, for instance, to the existence of a wide variety of opportunities. Many UAE entrepreneurs have, therefore, genuine difficulty in identifying a specific venture by applying rational criteria.

Biased business choice

Self-employment and small business is concentrated in most countries under review in trade. Egypt's small business sector is overwhelmingly trade-based (*Economist*, March 1999). Services provide, also, the backbone of small business in the UAE. Industry's contribution to small ventures is still relatively marginal. Another source of trouble is that the majority of these enterprises are "me too" enterprises or imitations of other businesses that proved to be successful. They are devoid of originality or innovation and are futile attempts to capitalize on what proved to be a success elsewhere.

Non-guided entry

Would be entrepreneurs are, for the greatest part, left to fight the battle on their own and are given nominal guidance when it comes to concept development, operationalization, and longer-term projection of the outcome. Feasibility assessment is regarded as the major effort while operationalization of the venture is, in reality, a more demanding task.

Finance

This is about the most common issue worldwide although it needs clarification when it comes to Arab countries. There are those where finance, especially venture capital, is nearly impossible (Egypt, for example) and those where it is accessible albeit with some strings attached (UAE, for example). The institutions are there but funds do not flow.

Conditions for exit

One seldom comes across an entrepreneur who has given the thought of failure any consideration while setting up the business. And it is not only giving it a thought but translating that into concrete scenarios of alternative possibilities. Choice of an exit vehicle is, in the majority of cases, vague at best.

Understanding and choosing technology

Entrepreneurs earn most of their technological knowledge during a period of paid employment. This guarantees a degree of understanding of the industry, but provides no guarantee that this is complete, or of proper assistance when it comes to choosing an appropriate one of the myriad of technologies available. Those without the advantage of this past experience are, it goes without saying, at great loss taking the right decision.

Survival barriers

Administrative and regulatory requirements

Demands of administrative or regulatory nature, initiated by a myriad of government agencies, have long been identified as a major strain for the small business entrepreneur. Cases are abundant and one has only to refer even to the popular press to confirm this.

No time to think of tomorrow

Small business owners, in Arab countries or elsewhere, confine most of their efforts to the removal of operational bottlenecks that emerge in the course of their daily conduct of business. The longer term picture is, in the majority of cases, an afterthought.

Where is the market information

Finding reliable market information and developing a realistic picture of the market the small business is facing is a serious survival barrier. The problem is probably the very narrow market share that the business is striving for, and that macro and aggregate data are really of limited use to a fractioned and narrow market segment.

Finances, again

Unbalanced capital structure, an inability to manage working capital, and undercapitalization are all problems common to small businesses. Both old and young bankrupt firms suffer this deficiency. This is compounded, in the Arab world, with an imperfect capital market or a market that lacks responsiveness to the needs of the small firm. Venture capital supply is way below demand and conditions attached are too inhibitive to stimulate genuine support for the small business firm. Add to that management failure and the commonly observed notion of a management that is unable to raise resources to pursue different financing options.

Unfair competition

Competition is tough as it is but there are times when an element of unfairness makes it impossible to deal with. The result is business failure. Unfairness arises from several sources; one common to several countries in the Middle East is market dominance by specific ethnic groups. The Chinese community dominates business in Malaysia, for example, a situation that the Malaysian government had to combat through juristic action. Asian communities dominate trade in East Africa, a situation that resulted in political repercussions. There is a likelihood that an element of this unfair competition exists in the UAE.

Technology shifts

The technology shifts we are currently witnessing in typical small business industries, such as printing, electric appliance assembly, services are, for many small entrepreneurs a jump in the dark. They may neither have the understanding of the new technology nor the resources to acquire it.

Firms in the UAE are exposed to the latest developments in technology and are under pressure to take the jump despite the cost and the risk involved in the process.

Exit barriers

Lack of alternatives

Exit is a luxury in economies where unemployment is discouraging school leavers idle in search of even a modest job. Rates of outright unemployment as well as disguised unemployment exceed, in several Arab countries, 25 percent of the workforce, conditions far from accommodating for a venture creator even if the venture is limping. Leaving the venture behind is, under these conditions, agonizing even if the price is hours of unpaid work!

The social stigma

Creating a business is an emotional process. Motivational forces play a major role at the creation stage. Failure makes mockery of all of that and translates it, in many societies, into a social stigma of failure. Arab cultures are high power distance cultures and this power distance magnifies the impact of failure. The decision for an entrepreneur in the UAE, as the author has witnessed, to lay a venture to rest is very difficult and emotionally charged.

Cost of exit

If exit were free, some entrepreneurs may have found it easy to take the decision. The trouble is that it does not come free and it bears, mostly, a heavy burden in terms of sunken fixed assets investment, costs of employee lay-off, and other complementary costs. Many entrepreneurs do not have the resources to cover all these outlays and some others may have debts to financial institutions that would almost forbid them from taking this step!

Potential for a restart

As we said earlier, 61 percent of failing entrepreneurs in the United States embark upon a new venture! It is common wisdom that it takes three failures for an entrepreneur to land a surviving venture. This requires flexibility, agility, versatility, and courage. Some of these traits are intrinsic while others are learned.

Types of sickness

There are three distinguishing types of sickness:

- Permanently recoverable. This is where the basic tenets or the core competencies of the business are solid and preserved. These could relate to a unique product, a unique technology, protected market niche, a strong business alliance, a viable management team, a dexterous work force.

• Nearly recoverable or recoverable under certain conditions. The nearly recoverable is a state where the core competences are being challenged but intervention could re-establish viability. It could also be a situation where the core competencies are not developed yet and they have to develop to sustain existence.

• Non-recoverable or "end game." where both the core competencies and the environmental conditions are hostile and a likelihood of a normal conduct of business is not really there/is absent. This could happen if demand for the industry's product collapses (competition, substitutes, cost, regulation, etc), the technology is not sustainable (costly, hazardous, too complex, etc), finance stream is cut permanently, etc.

The following Figure 6.2 represents the different states of sickness referred to above.

Empirical data do not allow a supportive analysis such as this within Arab countries. One can only speculate that the frequency of non-recovery is high and the disclosure of a non-recovery status is low. Cultural factors could have a profound impact on this state of affairs.

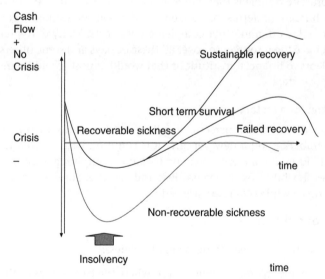

Figure 6.2   Typical states of sickness and recovery of small enterprise

Summary and conclusions

Small business does not, unfortunately, play the same role and demonstrate the same dominance in Arab countries as it does in several other parts of the world. The Propensity to Enterprise in the few Arab countries for which data are available is lower than those elsewhere and does not demonstrate the dynamic dimension observed in, for example, South and East Asia. Reasons vary, but they could relate to pre-entry flaws, precarious existence of those who enter, lack of tools for survival, and not knowing how to exit. Culture is a key factor too.

6.2   Bright and dark side of the Arab entrepreneur

The problem

Entrepreneurs, everywhere, have their bright and their dark sides. The problem, however, is the point of balance and where that point of balance leads. Research addressing this area is limited especially when it comes to the dark side. One of the classic attempts in this direction is Ketz De Vries's "the dark side of the entrepreneur" which is more than two decades old (Ketz De Vries, 1985). What he did was juxtapose the positive and less than positive sides of entrepreneurs in North America. His research on 38 of them from a wide range of American industries revealed them as achievement oriented, liking to take responsibility for decisions, and disliking repetitive work. He also found them to be visionary, creative, and have high levels of energy. But he equally found them to have strong personality traits to the extent of making them difficult people to work with. Their difficult characteristics included a need for control, a sense of distrust, desire for applause, and particular defenses.

Where do Arab entrepreneurs stand?

Nobody really knows. Research on Arab entrepreneurs is limited in scale and narrow in exposure. And exposing the dark side of the Arab entrepreneur is the last thing that could, understandably, occur to a researcher in search of a research topic within an Arab context. What follows, therefore, is an attempt at exploring this dark side but seeks balance by exposing the positive side as well. What the author did is explore the probabilities of occurrence of four parameters, two for "brightness" and two for "darkness." The brightness parameters related to achievement motivation and the locus of control. The dark parameters focused on the distrust of the environment and the propensity to enterprise. Judgmental samples of entrepreneurs, both practicing and potential, were taken from several Arab countries including Egypt and the United Arab Emirates. The samples represented both male and female entrepreneurs and potential entrepreneurs. A number of questionnaires related to the universally recognized key traits of entrepreneurs were completed by each country group. Results of these questionnaires were complemented by a parallel analysis of "macro" instruments as the propensity to enterprise and national culture dimensions.

Conceptual foundations of the analysis and the approach

This chapter relies on three conceptual frameworks: McClelland's, Hofstede's, and El Namaki's.

David McClelland's work on achievement motivation provided the base of the achievement motivation segment of the analysis. David McClelland is most noted for his work on human motivational needs which he has segmented into three (McClelland, 1961): achievement motivation (n-ach); authority/power motivation (n-pow); affiliation motivation (n-affil). The following analysis is based on the n-ach or the achievement motivation dimension of McClelland's analysis. This was measured, through a survey of a judgmental sample of entrant or practicing entrepreneurs, and compared to the level elsewhere.

Hofstede's work on culture's consequences (Hofstede, 1984) proved to be helpful in explaining several of the culture-related traits of the Arab entrepreneur. He views culture in terms of "dimensions" and identifies five dimensions: power distance, individualism, masculinity, uncertainty avoidance, and long-term orientation. Power distance focuses on the degree of equality, or inequality, between people in a country. Individualism relates to the degree the society reinforces individual or collective achievement and interpersonal relationships. Masculinity reflects the degree the society reinforces, or does not, the traditional masculine work role model of male achievement, control, and power. Uncertainty avoidance depicts the level of tolerance for uncertainty within the society. And, finally, long-term orientation focuses on the degree the society embraces, or does not embrace, long-term devotion to traditional, forward thinking values. Hofstede's Arab country coefficients for his five dimensions were helpful in explaining some of the elements of the darker side of the entrepreneur.

Finally, the authors own work on the Propensity to Enterprise or the relationship between self-employment and total employment within an economy supplied the conceptual framework for the propensity to enterprise analysis. The propensity to enterprise is a measure of entrepreneurial initiative that was explored for countries at different levels of economic growth and led to a number of relevant conclusions (El Namaki, 1990). The propensities to enterprise of several Arab countries were measured and incorporated into the assessment of some of the dark side parameters.

Results

The bright side

High motivation to achieve

Achievement motivation is the desire to achieve significant accomplishment, to master skills and ideas, to gain control, and to rapidly attain specific goals. The concept, as we said earlier, is rooted in David McClelland pioneering work on achievement-based motivational theory and models. McClelland's n-ach person is "achievement motivated" and therefore seeks achievement and attainment of realistic but challenging goals. He demonstrates a strong need for feedback on extent of achievement and progress as well as a need for a sense of accomplishment (McClelland, 1961).

McClelland firmly believed that achievement-motivated people are generally the ones who make things happen and get results, and that this extends to getting results through the organization of other people and resources, although as stated earlier, they often demand too much of those who work for them because they prioritize achieving the goal above the many varied interests and needs of their people.

An attempt at measuring the achievement motivation of a sample of Arab entrepreneurs and with the help of a recognized instrument (Ray, 1979) was done on three occasions. The first sample was of a number of women entrepreneurs in the United Arab Emirates. The second was a number of "entrant" entrepreneurs in Egypt. The third was a number of practicing entrepreneurs in Saudi Arabia. The results feature in the following Table 6.4. The mean of the achievement scores is, in all cases, somewhat higher than data once derived from, admittedly, older tests that were carried out with help of the same instrument, in the United Kingdom and Australia.

Table 6.4 Results of an achievement motivation test of a sample of women entrepreneurs in the UAE

Variable	Mean
The achievement motivation score for a judgmental sample of women entrepreneurs in Dubai, the United Arab Emirates (1)	35.9 (n = 10)
The achievement motivation score for a judgmental sample of entrepreneurs in Saudi Arabia (3)	36.6 (n = 11)
The achievement motivation score for a judgmental sample of potential entrepreneurs in Egypt (2)	33.9 (n = 62)
Achievement motivation score	
UK	32.5 (n = 100)
Australia (3)	31.4 (n = 95)

Notes:
1. Testing instrument is based on J.J. Ray (1979). It is a self report based on the completion of a questionnaire. Test was done in Sept 2004.
2. The same testing instrument. Test was done in Feb 2006.
3. Comparative scores are based on Ray's research

Strong internal locus of control

Locus of control is a personality construct referring to an individual's perception of the locus of events as determined internally by his/her own behavior or externally by fate, luck, or other external circumstances. The classification *internal locus* indicates that the person feels in control of events; *external locus* indicates that others are perceived to have that control. Persons with an internal locus of control see themselves as responsible for the outcomes of their own actions. These individuals often believe that they control their destiny, and are often observed to excel in educational or vocational realms. Someone with an external locus of control, on the other hand, sees environmental causes and situational factors as being more important than internal ones. These individuals would be more likely to see luck rather than effort as determining whether they succeed or fail in the future, and are more likely to view themselves as the victim in any given situation.

Three tests of locus of control were conducted among a sample of Arab entrepreneurs. They were based on an instrument developed in the United States (Pettijohn, 1999). The three samples were as as stated above. Results of all these tests are reproduced in Table 6.5 below.

The results point to a "healthy" dose of internal locus of control in Egypt and the United Arab Emirates and a "balanced" locus of control in the case of Saudi Arabia. The visible bias towards internal control in the

Table 6.5   Results of a locus of control test of a sample of entre-preneurs in Egypt, the UAE and Saudi Arabia*

Variable	Mean
Locus of control score for a sample of entrepreneurs in the United Arab Emirates	70 (n = 11)
Locus of control for a sample of entrepreneurs in Saudi Arabia	47 (n = 11)
Locus of control for a sample of entrepreneurs in Egypt	70 (n = 58)

Notes: * Testing instrument based on Pettijohn, 1999. A 65 to 80 score embodies an internal locus of control while a score ranging between the 40 and 60 points reflects a blend of the internal and the external locus of control. An 85 to 100 range would reflect a very strong internal locus of control

case of Egypt and the UAE as well as the balanced state in Saudi Arabia could be considered positive and a boon to private initiative.

The dark side

Distrust of the environment

Many entrepreneurs in the Arab countries are quick to express their distrust of their environment and demonstrate an unwillingness to view it in trustworthy terms. They express that in terms of attitude towards their fellow business colleagues, their government, their employees and, even, their customers. Anecdotal evidence abounds but we can get some hard empirical evidence from Hofstede's analysis of culture's dimensions and it consequences (Hofstede, 1984). Hofstede's landmark research identifies five cultural dimensions, or norms, and ranks countries according to a scale that he refers to as the Index. These cultural dimensions start with power distance and uncertainty avoidance and end with individualism, masculinity, and long-term orientation. Hofstede's specific analysis of Arab countries reveals a situation where power distance and uncertainty avoidance are high (an index of 80 and 68 respectively compared to a world average ranking of 51 and 64 also respectively) and individualism is low (38 compared to a world average ranking of 68). This implies an inequality in the distribution of power and wealth and a low level of tolerance for uncertainty and ambiguity within the society. It equally implies a basic distrust of ways and means of gaining power and distribution of wealth. And the low individualism

Table 6.6　Culture's dimensions index according to Hofstede

Culture's dimension	Arab countries index	Average world index	USA index
Power distance	80	51	40
Uncertainty avoidance	68	64	46
Individualism	38	68	91
Masculinity	53	51	62

Source: Hofstede, 1984

index translates into a close long-term commitment and absolute loyalty to the member "group", that is family, extended family, or extended relationships (Table 6.6).

Low propensity to enterprise

The propensity to enterprise is a measure of the inclination of individuals within a society to opt for the private initiative and independent economic performance of a business function. This was measured by relating the level of self-employment to the total volume of working population within the country in question. Measurement of this relationship has led to a number of interesting results (El Namaki, 1990). One of those is the existence of a range within which the propensity could fluctuate for a given level of country economic growth. Countries in the "developed market economy" range of the World Bank had a propensity range of 9–12 percent compared with countries with "developing economies" that scored 30–40 percent. Second is the existence of an inverse relationship between the stage of economic development of an economy and the level of propensity to enterprise. The higher the level of economic development the lower is the propensity.

Applying the propensity to enterprise to Arab countries was constrained by data. Arab countries for which data were available measured low along the propensity to enterprise scale. Sample data featuring in Table 6.7 below demonstrate a low propensity level in Egypt and a comparatively low propensity to enterprise in The West Bank and Gaza or Palestine (26.3 percent in 2003) and Tunisia (26.8 percent in 2003). Data were not available for countries where the relationship is of paramount economic (and even political) significance, such as Syria and the United Arab Emirates. Neither were data available for Saudi Arabia and the United Arab Emirates, the two countries where other surveys were conducted.

Table 6.7 The propensity to enterprise in selected Arab countries

Country/Year	1999 (%)	2003 (%)
Egypt	11.5	17.9
Tunisia	23.4	26.8
The West Bank and Gaza or Palestine	18.7	27.8

Source: ILO Bureau of Statistics. Working population and "own account" data are drawn from the International Labor Office database on labor statistics operated by the ILO Bureau of Statistics. ILO defines an Own-account worker as a person who operates his or her own economic enterprise, or engages independently in a profession or trade, and hires no employees.

Discussion

Why is there a contrast between high achievement motivation and low propensity to enterprise?

There exists a curious contrast between the level of achievement motivation of the sample that was surveyed in Egypt and the level of propensity to enterprise that emerges from the employment data of the country. While the sample may not represent the entire population, the contrast is striking and could suggest, at some risk of course, the existence of significant barriers in the way of those who opt for private initiative as an occupational career. What it actually says is that there are individuals with the desire to achieve who can not match this desire with an actual act of achievement!

Is there a "clash of enterprise"?

An explanation for the low propensity to enterprise in Arab countries may also be found in the unique attributes of the culture dimensions of Hofstede. The disparity would be vivid if one is to compare Arab country indices with those of the United States. Free market norms and values in the United States are leading to a culture of high individualism, low uncertainty avoidance, and low power distance. This strong contrast between Arab countries' attributes and those of the US could explain the less than optimum level of the propensity to enterprise. The US propensity to enterprise levels are compatible with the norms introduced into earlier work (El Namaki, 1990) and more recent data support this notion (Table 6.8).

Table 6.8   Arab and USA attributes of culture's dimension index

Culture's dimension	Arab countries index	USA index
Power distance	80	40
Uncertainty avoidance	68	46
Individualism	38	91
Masculinity	53	62

Source: Hofstede, 1984

Will there be change?

Change may be holding the answer to the state of enterprise in Arab countries. Figures provided earlier reflect a tangible increase in the level of the propensity to enterprise between the two years of observation (1999 and 2003). Other relevant indicators such as the flow of FDI in Arab countries, the start of an active venture capital industry, and the emergence of Arab MNCs will certainly boost this process of enterprise. One may also add here that the analysis touched upon the formal sector which is only a slice of the entire picture. There exists a thriving informal sector in all countries referred to in this analysis, and this may tip the balance towards a "healthier" and more encouraging view.

Summary and conclusions

The trouble with entrepreneurs everywhere having a bright and their dark sides is the difficulty in finding the point of balance and deciding where it leads. Research addressing this area is limited especially when it comes to the dark side. One of the classic attempts in this direction is Ketz De Vries's "the dark side of the entrepreneur" which is more than two decades old (Ketz de Vries, 1985). What he did was juxtapose the positive and less than positive sides of entrepreneurs in North America. His research on 38 entrepreneurs from a wide range of industries revealed them as achievement oriented, liking to take responsibility for decisions, and disliking repetitive work. He also found them to be visionary, creative, and have high levels of energy. But he equally found them to have strong personality traits to the extent of making them difficult people to work with. Their difficult characteristics included: a need for control, a sense of distrust, desire for applause, and particular defenses.

Research on Arab entrepreneurs is limited and the issue of "dark" or "bright" side of entrepreneurial initiative has, to the best of the author's knowledge, never been addressed. In this chapter, we have tried to redress the balance.

What the author did is explore the probabilities of occurrence of four parameters two for "brightness" and two for "darkness". The brightness parameters related to achievement motivation and the locus of control. The darkness parameters focused on the distrust of the environment and the low propensity to enterprise. All four parameters could raise questions related to the contrast between a high achievement motivation and low propensity to enterprise and the cultural roots of the low propensity to enterprise as well.

The article is based, conceptually on works by McClelland on achievement motivation, Hofstede on Culture's consequences and El Namaki on the Propensity to Enterprise.

7
Capital and Finance

7.1   Would venture capital work in the GCC?

The problem

Venture capital and private equity investment are fairly new phenomena in GCC countries. The initiatives are recent and the learning curve is yet to unfold. Small business relies, traditionally, and the GCC states are no exception, on savings, personal loans, and family reserves, contributions by friends and associates, and, venture capital. Venture capital is a provider of small business equity input in the United States. This is usually complemented by commercial bank loans, loans by financial institutions, and loans made by the entrepreneur himself. So venture capital contribution to small business finance is narrow and the road to it is bumpy. Conditions are stringent and the process is exhausting. Critical noises are loud and experience in other emerging economies is far from encouraging.

How do things look in the GCC states?

In this chapter we analyze generic small business finance needs and what venture capital, or private equity investment, really does. Then we identify sources of venture capital in the Gulf States and define their parameters. Next we assess the likely small business demand for venture capital and the conditions for a successful acquisition.

Throughout, we are comparative in approach. Sound venture capital practice in countries with a solid track record as is the United States, is taken as a point of reference. Experience of other emerging economies such as Thailand and Malaysia is also cited.

The article is based on a number of sources. Prime among those is data on venture capital practice in the country dominating the venture capital market, i.e. the USA. To this was added data on venture capital resources and experience in the GCC. The little research that was done on the issue at a national or a regional scale was also consulted. Expert opinion has also been sought. The terms venture capital and private equity finance are used interchangeably in this article.

Small business finance, the general picture

Small business finance patterns vary according to the stage of economic growth of the country and the state of the economy at that specific point of time. Informal finance is dominant in emerging economies while formal finance venues are more likely to assume a greater role in developed economies. In a mature situation such as that of the United States self-funding or equity is the lifeblood of the entrepreneur. They, the entrepreneurs, provided, for example, 65.8 percent of the start-up capital in 2003 (GEM report, 2005) and venture capital seems to be the venue of last resort, according to the same report.

Debt is, of course, a secondary source of finance to these entrepreneurs. This is provided, in the US by banks, financial institutions, or the entrepreneur. Data reveal that the most important institutional supplier of credit to small firms in the United States is commercial banks. They supplied 57 percent of all small business outstanding credit in 1998. This compared to 12 percent supplied by the owner and 11 percent supplied by finance companies (USA Small Business Administration, 2005).

Surprisingly, an overwhelming 88 percent of America's 500 fastest growing private companies never received financing from a venture capital entity. In contrast, 33 percent of the same 500 companies raised start-up capital "by tapping the assets of family and friends" (GEM report 2004). Growth in size of assets of the small firm is also likely to result in a growth in equity. The majority of small firms finance their asset growth through equity financing (and retained earnings) rather than through debt financing.

Why venture capital?

Venture capital is an investment medium that fills important investment gaps:

- A start up gap;
- A growth gap;
- A turnaround gap;
- A restructuring gap.

These gaps can be difficult to cover through conventional finance instruments. Start ups are too weak to command the necessary "respect" when addressing a financial institution. Growth requires a sharing of outlook and vision that may not be easy to materialize. Turnaround requires courage and a risk-taking attitude that are not common among conventional institutions. And finally restructuring requires a long-term commitment to the firm or industry that may not be easy to muster.

By providing this gap-filling function, venture capital plays a vital role in enhancing the investment potential of an economy, a potential that is enhanced by economic growth, development strategies, and windfall gains. The economy (GDP) of the UAE is growing by more than 10 percent per year and this is creating demand-induced growth opportunities. The development strategy of the UAE spells out massive expansion in key industries (tourism, real estate, financial services, and IT) as well as a strong external orientation of the economy as a whole, and these are creating opportunities. Also oil price fluctuations are creating windfall gains and those, in their turn, induce opportunities.

How venture capital works

Let us recall that venture capital is "Money made available for investment in innovative enterprises or research, especially in high technology, in which both the risk of loss and the potential for profit may be considerable" (*The American Heritage Dictionary*). It is also referred to as "funds invested or available for investment in a new or unproven business enterprise" (*Random House Unabridged Dictionary*, 1997). The common element and the important thread here is high risk taking and the willingness to input funds in situations where returns could be high but could equally be low or not exist at all.

Venture capital and private equity funds are really "pools" of investor funds put together in order to exploit exceptional opportunities. For the investor to be invited into those "pools" there must be conditions. Among these are the following:

- The private equity organization must have a strong and successful track record;
- The team should be creditable and their industry experience and ability to add value are beyond question;
- There should be a sound system for opportunity evaluation and risk management;

- The "fund" should be clear in messages presented to the outside world and what it is out to achieve;
- The "fund" should have clear and explicit "exit" or "harvest" plans for the venture it gets involved in.

Let us also recall that venture capital and private equity funds finance small startups and early stage businesses as well as businesses in "turn around" situations. These investments can take the form of either equity participation, or a combination of equity participation and debt obligation – often with convertible debt instruments that become equity if a certain level of risk is exceeded. In most cases, the venture capitalist becomes part owner of the new venture. The scope is usually narrow and venture capitalists are typically interested in making few large investments, due to the manpower needed to support each investment (recruiting and board seats).

Finally, it is good to remember that a small business is only considered fit for venture capital financing if it:

- has a high growth prospect within a specific time frame;
- has a product or service with a competitive edge;
- is supported by strong management team;
- can demonstrate a proved track record.

Also those investors in venture capital and private equity organizations are growing increasingly careful and there is a general hesitation towards investing in initial fundraising. In this environment, a sophisticated investor will take into account a range of factors in evaluating the opportunity. These include:

- The private equity organization track record;
- The credibility of the team, their industry experience and ability to add value;
- The soundness of the private equity organization systems, risk management, and governance procedures;
- The clarity and substance of the key messages presented.

Processes involved in the venture capital fund mobilization and disbursement as described above feature in the following Figure 7.1. Returns and flows to each player, i.e. cash, return on investment, and cash flows are demonstrated as well.

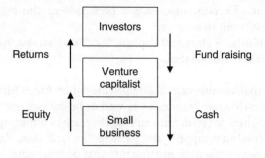

Figure 7.1   The buildup of the venture capital process

What is the experience?

Over the past two decades the venture capital industry in the United States has experienced dramatic growth. Annual inflows into venture funds have expanded from virtually zero in the mid 1970s to a high of US$105 billion in 2000. Disbursements by these funds into portfolio companies have displayed almost as great a growth. Many of the most visible new firms over the past decades – including massive multinationals such as Apple Computer, Intel, Lotus, and Microsoft – have been backed by venture capital funds. This growth has led to increasing attention to the venture capital industry from the popular press, executives of major corporations, and policy-makers worldwide.

Yet despite this expansion and attention, problems haunt the industry especially when it comes to small business finance. And experience varies. The GEM (Global Entrepreneurship Monitor) report refers to an actual decline in venture capital contribution to small business finance in the United States. It quotes a number of parameters to support this conclusion. These include relationship between venture capital and GDP (declined to 0.2 percent from 0.5 percent) and the number of companies receiving venture capital (declined also from 18,569 to 18,247), for all GEM countries taken together between 2000 and 2001 (GEM, 2002).

By far the rarest source of capital for nascent entrepreneurs is classic venture capital. So rare is it, that even in the US, which has more than two-thirds of the total venture capital in the entire world (74% VC among G7 nations in 2003), far fewer than one in ten thousand new ventures receive their initial financing from VC firms. (GEM 2005)

The venture capital industry in the United States is also said to be maturing and needs major restructuring. There are claims that the industry is far from organized and that practice within the industry does not follow a norm or a system (Spreng, 2005). The industry is secretive and is difficult to monitor. There is a lack of meaningful performance data and large discrepancies in published benchmarks (SCM, 2005).

The venture capital industry is not faring much better in Asia. Reasons are many but prime among them is the lack of history or culture of venture capitalism.

> Asian entrepreneurs are not too familiar with the practices and norms that U.S. venture capitalists expect. And Western VCs, for their part, often don't take the time to educate the entrepreneurs or to develop the sorts of personal relationships that are still highly valued in many Asian countries. (Knowledge@Wharton, 2004)

Asian entrepreneurs find some of the clauses of the legal agreements that venture investors use to set out the conditions for their investments, offensive. They interpret the contracts as a sign that the investor doesn't trust them rather than as a normal means of doing business. Some Asian entrepreneurs also don't understand why venture capitalists want to be heavily involved with their companies, checking in weekly, and participating in board deliberations.

It is also worth stressing here that the venture capital industry nearly collapsed in the Far East as a result of the Asian currency crisis of 1997, and although a revival is about to take place many of the cruel lessons of the 1990s are still fresh in mind.

Is there venture capital in the GCC area?

The Arab capital market is still in an "infant industry." The market is low on institutional investors, highly capitalized companies, foreign investors, ethical codes, enforceable laws, liquid stocks, and flexible regulations. Venture capital and private equity investment are, to all appearances, one of the least developed vehicles. No wonder that the first attempts in this direction are met with excitement.

It is the author's view that there are three types of venture capital and private equity financing in the GCC:

1. General finance;
2. Shariah-bound finance;
3. Outreach finance.

General venture capital and private equity finance is that type that is regionally generated and neutrally administered. What this means is that the resources of this type of finance are raised locally and that the management of the funds is done within a national or regional context (no technical link to foreign investment firms). The reason for this distinction is that non-Middle East involvement brings with it measures and criteria that change the character of the service and the nature of the product.

Shariah-bound finance is based on the Islamic foundation of investment. These are spelled out in relevant documents.

Outreach finance is provided by multinational investment organizations and banks, as an extension of a global function. The overall umbrella here is global and whatever is done in the region is done within a global perspective. This does lead to different market segmentation, different product features, and different service criteria.

Here are some examples:

Case 1: The venture capital Bank of Bahrain

This is a Shariah-bound venture capital fund approved by the Bahrain Monetary Agency in May 2005. A Shariah board is set in order to explore proposal compliance with Shariah principles and certifies that the proposed investment is within the norms identified by Shariah. The bank will invest in "strong undervalued, finance-seeking small to medium enterprises (SMEs) with market and revenue growth potential." It will also invest in real estate being one of the especially attractive investment opportunities in the area.

VC Bank is linked to an American venture capital firm, Global Emerging Markets Group (GEM Group), as a technical partner. GEM Group is active with deal origination, advisory, merger, acquisition, corporate finance, and turn-around firms with a strong focus on emerging markets.

Case 2: Injazat technology

Injazat Technology Fund is also a Shariah-bound fund. It has a US$50 million capital that it operates in strict compliance with Shariah principles. It targets technology companies within the MENA region. The Fund was initiated by the Islamic Corporation for the Development of the Private Sector (ICD), an affiliate of the Islamic Development Bank (IDB) and by Gulf Finance House (GFH), in partnership with Dubai

Islamic Bank, Saudi Economic and Development Company (SEDCO), and Iran Foreign Investment Corporation (IFIC).

Case 3: HSBC private equity middle east L.P.

HSBC fund is what I call an "outreach fund." This is a US$118 million fund that has been created specifically for investment in the GCC. Out of these US$118 million, US$85 million has been drawn from regional institutional sources. This HSBC fund is focused on private equity opportunities with established profitable businesses, often where there is scope to assist in taking the company public on the region's stock markets, or to expand the business in the GCC and beyond. Key decision factors are strong management and sound growth prospects.

There are other examples, some using *bona fide* venture capital funds, also those we may term "quasi" venture capital funds. To the first category belongs Ithmar, a venture capital fund under construction. To the second belong many other initiatives. Some of these are undertaken by benevolent well-endowed individuals in search of an opportunity to either invest in lucrative investments (real estate, for example) or fulfill a social responsibility. Some others are extensions of global venture capital investments elsewhere. Yet others are instruments of corporate strategies and, as such, are not private equity either in spirit or behavior.

The sum of all of that does not constitute a mature venture capital or a private equity industry at best.

What are small business finance needs in the area?

Starters need finance whether they are in the GCC or elsewhere. Experience in Dubai is illustrative of the narrow possibilities and the few alternatives open to them. More than 80 percent of graduates from a recent program on small business put external finance as a condition for the fulfillment of their business plans. They also narrowed the span of availability of this finance to a few institutions, including two quasi government organizations (Al Tomoh and Sheik Moh Ben Rashid Foundation). These are organizations that are ready and willing to provide financial support in the form of loans under certain conditions and with strings attached. Prime among these is a sound and defendable business plan, something that is not within reach of every aspiring entrepreneur. Al Tomooh, for example, which is a financial scheme designed to support small businesses provides medium to long-term loans up to AED 2.0 million. Loan repayment should start from the second year of operations and extend over a maximum of eight years. An interest-free grace period of three years is granted.

Will venture capital respond to small business needs in the area?

Introduction of the venture capital concept in the GCC is positive and long overdue. Lack of equity input is a major constraint for many an entrepreneur and reliance on conventional sources of finance is often mentioned as a prime bottleneck in the growth of the small business sector.

The question, however, is how effective will those institutions be and will they provide a genuine answer to the existing need? Let us remember that venture capital and private equity venture are dependent on three prime inputs: capital, management, and opportunities. If they are only selectively there, we have a problem. Experience elsewhere casts a shadow over the availability of those components and the way they are managed.

It is the author's contention that venture capital attempts within the GCC will face volume, scale, scope, and texture constraints. There are, essentially, significant gaps in:

- Awareness of the intricacies of venture capital finance.
- Experience at fulfilling venture capital finance requirements.
- Venture capital culture.
- Proper venture capital-based methods for project evaluation and assessment.
- Methods for reconciling mundane Shariah demands with the global requirements of venture finance.
- Venture capital resources.
- New venture management teams.
- Availability of unique high risk but high potential ventures.
- Complementary finance.
- Legal framework for venture capital operations.
- Exit channels for venture capital investments (the harvest option).
- Availability of exceptional risk/reward businesses.

These are critical barriers and the likelihood that the industry will be able to cope with them in the short term is low.

Where will growth in venture capital come from in the GCC?

Although capital and liquidity are abundant in the UAE the size of venture capital resources remains very modest. Time is bound to bring about a tangible growth in these resources. Sources of this growth could be:

- Individual assets;
- Government investment funds;
- Domestic financial institutions;
- Sharia-based financial institutions;
- Foreign venture capital firms;
- Foreign investment institutions.

The question really is who will play a prime role and who will be relegated to the bottom ranks. Individuals are not used to the venture capital concept yet and contrary to the situation in, say, the United States, the "wealth comradeship" that lies at the heart of individual fund pooling arrangements in the United States might not work here. Culture is not conducive to that (at least in the short run). Government will, very likely, and in the medium term, play a major role in creating venture capital funds that are responsive to the specific needs of the market (national start ups specifically). Foreign venture capital firms and foreign investment institutions will enter, undoubtedly, but will rely on joint ventures more than anything else. They will also focus on foreign owned and foreign run companies.

Sharia-based financial institutions could become a vital contributor to the venture capital resource base provided the concept is made a bit more "mundane."

Domestic financial institutions are a bit "timid" about venture capital.

What to do

It is the author's contention that several measures are needed urgently in order to guarantee the effectiveness of this vital instrument of small business finance:

- **Promoting the concept of venture capital**. Several promotional vehicles should be used to explain to the potential consumer what venture capital is and what it is not. These could include public seminars or specific training sessions. Articles exploring the issue could also be placed in relevant publications.

- **Formulating a legal framework for venture capital use**. Proposals should be formulated for the legal boundaries of venture capital operators, what could be done and what should be avoided. These should relate to the rights and obligations of the venture capitalist and the consequences of malfunctioning of the system.

- **Mobilizing resources**. Volumes of funds mobilized in the venture capital initiatives announced lately are modest compared to practice elsewhere and, of course, market needs. An attempt at getting novel entrants, institutional investors, for example, to participate in the effort and increase the scale would represent a step forward.

- **Complying with Shariah requirements**. This is a critical issue and some serious work is needed into how to make an investment proposal congruent with Shariah requirements. Without this many investment proposals may not qualify for venture capital support, at least the type we are discussing here.

- **Developing venture capital infrastructure**. That is, the non-capital inputs into the venture capital system. These would include professional management teams, technology, sources, R&D labs, etc. All of these must be in place for opportunities to emerge and be exploited.

- **Creating a market for ventures**. Venture capital is a fairly short-term affair and venture capitalists are always on the look out for an opportunity for a "harvest." Unless there is a market for ventures where they exchange hands in a structured and organized manner, one of the prime premises of venture capital is not there.

- **Developing venture capital administrative access mechanism**. Completing the requirements of venture capital funds is an exhausting process that requires knowledge and skill. Some focused training is required for potential start ups and for small business entrepreneurs to work with this mechanism.

Summary and conclusions

Venture capital is a by-product of the free market-based capital market mechanism. It makes a significant contribution to small business finance in mature economies such as that of the United States. It rewards risk and demonstrates an ability to respond to opportunities. It is also culture-bound. The phenomenon is, however, new to many countries including the GCC, and views on its effectiveness are not uniform. Experience in Asia has revealed the existence of cultural and operational constraints, some as serious as to undermine the potential of the vehicle altogether. The industry is also under pressure in the

United States with claims of disorganization and lack of a uniform approach. In the GCC countries, a firm foundation of venture capital operations is yet to be created. This would require some major steps, including venture capital promotion, creation of a legal base, resource mobilization, venture market creation, and shariah compliance.

7.2   Venture capital: What can Arab institutions learn from the Chinese?

The problem

Venture capital is an infant industry in China. It is following the trails of Foreign Direct Investment (FDI) and is only now beginning to show some presence. FDI was and still is a major success in the country. At an average of US$45 billion a year over a decade, it penetrated almost each and every Chinese industrial branch and provided the prime driving force for the automotive, computing, steel, and even shipping industries. It could not, however, be the same thing to all people. It turned out to be an instrument that best suits the large and powerful and not the small and weak. Those small and weak businesses had to find their solace in venture capital and private equity funds. They were ready to listen, tailor, and tune. They are geared to the risk and investment requirements of the small entrepreneur and they accommodate the spirit of uncertainty and failure that is typical for this type of business.

Venture capital and private equity placement practice started only in the mid-1980s in China. It had a difficult childhood. There were problems of concept, environment, institutions, and practice. It nevertheless grew and innovated and this is the focus of what follows where we identify products and practices that are common within the Chinese venture capital industry but could be regarded as unique within other environments. We go further to assess the possibility of transferring some of those unique products and practices to the Middle East.

The arguments here rely on published material on the Chinese venture capital industry on the one hand and a series of interviews that the author had with venture capital operators, actual and potential, within and outside China. We also refer to the relevant experience of venture capital elsewhere in Asia.

Structure of the Chinese venture capital industry

As we said earlier, venture capital is an "infant industry" in China. Its short history started in the mid-1980s when the Chinese government decided to develop the high-tech sector. Most of the initial efforts failed. The China New Technology Start-up Investment Company, one of the well-known venture capital firms in China, went bankrupt in 1997. In the mid-1990s and early 2000 people began, gradually, to understand and accept the concepts of knowledge economy, high-tech industries, and venture capital. The year 1992 saw the introduction of the first foreign venture capital fund. A national regulation for foreign venture capital firms was introduced in 2001. And 2003 saw the introduction of a national regulation permitting foreign venture capital firms to raise local funds and manage them on a LLP basis.

There are more than 300 venture capital firms in China today. Only a little fewer than half of those are actively investing. And out of those that are active, about 60 percent are capitalized entirely by sources within mainland China. Data covering the first half of 2005 reveal that 53 percent of total venture capital investments in China has been in information technology companies, while 11 percent went into traditional sectors (Zero2ipo data, 2005). Total venture capital investment in China in 2004, including non-US firms, reached US$1.27 billion, up 28 percent from 2003.

Foreign involvement in the venture capital industry of China is recent and limited in scale (see following Table 7.1). Many Western venture capitalists struggle with language and cultural barriers especially the notion that business is a by product of personal relationships rather than other criteria (Buckman, 2005).

Table 7.1   China venture capital industry size

Variable/Year	'97	'98	'99	'00	'01	'02	'03
New (registered) venture capital firms	15	21	40	102	45	39	36
Total number of registered venture capital firms	39	60	100	202	247	296	332
Foreign venture capital firms							41
Joint ventures							18

Source: zero2ipo Venture Capital Research Center (China)

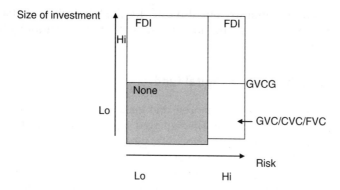

Figure 7.2 The opportunity in the Chinese venture capital industry

Notes: GVC: Government venture capital; CVC: Corporate venture capital; FVC: Foreign venture capital

The striking factor about the structure of the venture capital industry in China is that it demonstrates the same "strategic gap" the industry demonstrates elsewhere. It is still far from addressing the needs of small business in "traditional" sectors. Figure 7.2 illustrates that. While Foreign Direct Investment (FDI) is taking care of large investment at almost all levels of risk, all venture capital varieties in the country are addressing the high tech/high risk category and leaving behind the low or medium risk ventures in more "traditional" industries. This is an opportunity that foreign venture capital firms could explore.

China's unique venture capital products and practices

Government as enabler

Government has played a central role in the development of the Chinese venture capital industry. Government realized that venture capital was a key factor in the development of the high-tech industry in the United States and wanted to emulate that example. Linking science to technological development became a government objective and a vision that the Chinese government built into its development plans. The State Council, the State Planning Commission, and the Chinese Communist Party leadership all endorsed this notion and stimulated creation of the mechanisms that would implement this strategy (White *et al.*, 2002).

Unique products

The Chinese venture capital industry knows forms of venture capital organizations that are not very common elsewhere. These novel forms help support the industry but also cater for the "strategic gap" that we have referred to earlier (the low investment-low risk category within Figure 7.2).

The university venture capital fund

This has been established, financed, and managed by a single university. There are now many of them. They emerged in large numbers in 2000, and have continued to thrive ever since. They have, of course, strengths and weaknesses. To the strengths belong the fact that they build their venture capital portfolio on their inner prowess (Chinese Academy of Science, for example), their access to good and relevant information, their good market positioning, their proximity to a natural breeding ground of entrepreneurs, and, finally, their close cooperation with the corporate sector.

As to the weaknesses, the prime one is limited investment funds as most of these are created through channels other than government education grants or government budgets. Yet another weakness is the process of management of the fund itself.

Corporate venture capital funds

These are venture capital funds created by corporations either private or state owned. The first emerged in the early 1990s but they represent the majority today. Beijing High Tech VC and Beijing VC are the largest. Management is drawn from securities firms and banks. Newly listed companies with abundat cash belong to their ranks today (11 percent of listed companies have VC subsidiaries (2001 data)). They have, of course, pros and cons. The pros include business opportunity roots and the fact that new business opportunities are easy to come by. Add to that a professional management that knows what it is doing.

As to the cons they center on the quasi government tint that most of these companies have.

Provincial government venture capital fund

These fund finance direct and "obvious" opportunities identified, mostly, by the provincial government in the course of conducting its business. The difference with the other alternatives is the opportunity identification process and link to the provincial government.

The prime problem with these funds is their management. It is drawn from government ranks, and that is not always the best source for management quality. Government control over these organizations is also weak. These organizations are strong, however, when it comes to involvement. The direct involvement in and direct control by the provincial government does create an element of supervision that is conducive to good performance.

Managed intervention

Chinese venture capital firms are less active in their monitoring of the financed venture than venture capital firms in, say, the United States. Frequency of financial reporting is less than that demanded by foreign venture capital firms. In China and elsewhere, management is allowed far more freedom of decision making than otherwise is the case, incremental capital input is less frequent, contingency financing or financing based on achievement of benchmarks is also less likely, and supportive services (such as consultancy advice, for example) are limited and narrow in scope.

This all adds up to a looser, "laissez fair" attitude that could, in the author's view, induce a better environment for venture conduct.

What can we learn from the Chinese?

There is a lot to be learned from the Chinese experience, despite the short term and the continuous experimentation. Let us consider the following:

- **The role of government as an enabler**. There is room for government to take a leading role in the creation of venture capital funds and the encouragement of these institutions. This is especially relevant when it comes to investment in leading high-tech initiatives that are directly tied to individual innovation.
- **Creating university-linked venture capital funds**. Key universities in the UAE could demonstrate initiative, let alone entrepreneurship, by creating venture capital funds that would act and behave like their Chinese counterparts. The UAE University, the University of Sharja, and the Sheik Zeid University are all in a position to do so. A UAE University venture capital fund could go a long way towards encouraging innovation, boosting the spirit of entrepreneurship among students and faculty, and playing a role in the process of economic growth of the country.
- **Corporate endorsement of venture capital as a medium for entrepreneurship**. Large corporations such as EMAAR have grown

beyond the simple performance of a business function. They have become societal institutions with a social responsibility. Part of that social responsibility, if one is to disregard self-interest briefly, is the creation of a fertile ground for entrepreneurship and risk taking. What better way to do that than to create a dedicated venture capital fund to that specific goal.

- **Creating "soft" venture capital funds.** There is room for the creation of "soft" venture capital funds or funds supported by free management advice, incubation facilities, and technology transfer facilities. Venture capital organizations are known for their "harshness" and this probably explains the Chinese approach where government venture capital is supported by a host of other "soft" or low cost services. Why would not we create venture capital funds directly linked to the Science Park and industrial parks program? And grant those who would gain venture capital support softer terms of access to the services of those science parks?

- **Creating and adjusting the venture capital legal framework.** As we said earlier, the Chinese have spent considerable time trying to "perfect" their venture capital legal infra-structure. And when a law deemed insufficient they corrected it or amended it in order to conform to the specific needs of the market place. We need in the UAE three specific laws: a law on venture capital partnerships, a law on venture capital management, and a law on venture marketing or "retailing."

Summary and conclusions

The venture capital industry is a new phenomenon in China. It started only in the mid 1980s and had a difficult childhood. There were problems of concept, of environment, of institutions, and of practice. It nevertheless grew and innovated and this is the focus here. We have identified the main framework of the industry as it operates in China today and referred to three areas of innovation: the government as enabler, new forms of venture capital funds (university-linked, corporate born, provincial government started). We concluded that there is a lot to learn from the Chinese experience. There is a room for government facilitation within the industry in the UAE, for universities in the UAE to create their own venture capital funds, for large corporations to endorse the concept and for a bold initiative along the legal front.

8
Strategic Behavior

8.1   Family businesses in the Gulf States, a blessing or a challenge?

The problem

Family businesses are abundant in Arab countries. Gulf States are no exception. They compensate for the rather weak small business framework, the fragile stock markets, and the dominant government-owned enterprises. This is very much the case in countries as different as Morocco and Libya in North Africa, and Kuwait and Bahrain in the Gulf. Roots of family- firm dominance in Arab countries lie deep in Arab history and culture. The family was the foundation upon which networks were created and relationships established. The situation today is that where family firms represent around 92 percent of privately-held companies in the UAE. There were, in 2006, for example, 30,769 family-owned businesses in Dubai among the 56,374 totally registered with the Chamber of Commerce (Dubai Chamber of Commerce and Industry data; *Khaleeg Times*, 2006)

Though generally conducive to the purpose, family firms could be weak. Their approach to management, strategy formulation, human resource mobilization, and succession could be questioned. Their visions are, occasionally, blurred. Their ability to carry the banner into the future is not always evident.

The following pages deal with the underlying structure of family firms in the Gulf States; the approach is case-based. The ultimate objective is to answer three questions: how dominant are those firms, how do they formulate strategies, and how likely are they to meet the challenges of the years to come? A broad picture of family firm elsewhere is first provided.

Family businesses, the broad picture

Family-owned businesses feature heavily in almost every economy. There is ample evidence to that effect.

They contribute significantly to the total number of enterprises in the United States and Europe. The figure for the United States is 10 percent while that for France is 32 percent, England and Germany 30 percent. (McKinsey, 2007) (See Figure 8.1). Only 40 percent of family-owned businesses survive to the second generation, 12 percent to the third, and 3 percent to the fourth in the United States (*Boston Globe*, May 4, 2003). Nearly 40 percent of family businesses in America should have been passing the reigns to the next generation within a five year period (*Business Week*, August 11, 2003).

Family-firm problems, and opportunities, in both the United States and Europe, are familiar. They touch upon time allocated to management of the venture, priorities given to profits versus family affairs, motivation of non-family members, personal family battles fought within a business context, excessive employment of family members, and competency and fitness of family members for the functions they perform within the family firm.

The issue of succession is fundamental in family firms and receives, therefore, considerable attention. If offspring are to work in the family business, then three questions must be answered. First, does the child have an interest in the family business, or other aspirations? Second, is the child qualified? Third, how should the child be prepared for the family business? Recent evidence shows that family businesses managed by the eldest son fare significantly poorer on measurements like productivity, market share, sales growth, and market valuation compared to those run by outside executives (*Gulf News*, 2007). Family firms are distinctive

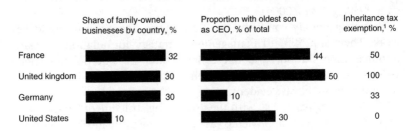

	Share of family-owned businesses by country, %	Proportion with oldest son as CEO, % of total	Inheritance tax exemption,[1] %
France	32	44	50
United kingdom	30	50	100
Germany	30	10	33
United States	10	30	0

Figure 8.1 Family firms share and management

Note: [1] For typical midsize family-owned business valued at >$10 million
Source: Stephen et al., The Mckinsey Quarterly, 6 Oct, 2007

in that they have to manage their business as well as their family relationships. In order to manage growth it is important that the right members of the family are chosen to manage different aspects of the business. Succession management then becomes a question of ability as opposed to the cultural norm of "eldest son."

A family firm is typically, and regardless of country, a firm where majority ownership is in the hands of the "family" (more than 50 percent of share capital under normal circumstances). It is also a firm where family members do the management and have been doing that for several generations. Their business tends to have a core focus and members of the family are usually involved in the day to day running of operations.

The family firm concept recognizes what one may term the "The Family Office" or an organization developed to manage and support the financial needs and management resources of a family group. Tasks performed by this office include actual management of member companies, structuring of the assets and investment and, occasionally, trusteeship.

Some measure of application of the family office concept exists in GCC countries.

Family firms could grow and prosper. Some of them could develop into powerful multinationals with operations across the globe. Examples include William Clarke & Sons (Ireland) which was founded in 1739 to manufacturer linen and still does so. And Villeroy & Bosch (Germany) which was founded in 1748 to manufacture porcelain and still does so also. Both firms are managed by the founding families.

Family businesses in the Gulf States

GCC family businesses are important entities in terms of size and contribution to the economy. They are predominantly large economic institutions with a key role in managing strategic sectors ranging from services to construction, trade and manufacturing. They have in this way tangible impact on output, employment, productivity, and the overall economic stability of the countries involved. GCC family businesses tend to differ in many ways from the global picture drawn above. Areas of divergence include the following:

- Businesses have short history that hardly extends beyond a few decades and often is managed and administered by the first generation
- Families strategies are "reactive" instead of "facilitating." Put differently their decisions are really a reflection of the rich opportunity environment within the area rather their own search for opportunities.

- The same abundant availability of capital and opportunities create an environment of disregard for core competency or the identification of a Strategic SCA Competitive advantage. The result is heterogeneous portfolios and a wide scatter of businesses within one and the same entity. They are probably true "conglomerates" in the North American sense.
- Families vary in terms of approach to the day to day management of their businesses. Some are heavily involved, others are not. The rationale is not clear and one feels inclined to relate it to contingency and situational criteria.
- The family is heavily involved in the selection of those executives who will eventually run their companies.
- Several large families with sizable portfolios act more as asset manager than operator. But this applies to those with a sizable volume of investment.

Family firms in the GCC have been performing well in terms of growth and returns. Actual data are difficult to come by but judgmental evidence is abundant. They face, however, challenges. Some of these originate from within the family itself, some others relate to the surrounding environment, and the rest are exposed to the globalization forces engulfing the area.

Case studies

The following are cases selected to illustrate the conceptual and operational framework outlined above. The first case demonstrates the process of converting a modest single industry family firm into a conglomerate. The second attends to the issue of top management and the making of a top executive of a family firm.

Case 1: The making of a family conglomerate

The first case is of a conglomerate that grew out of a modest family start up. Names and titles are withheld. The family office started operations in 1969 and was set up by the founder who had professional health sector roots. His start was a medical equipment trading company but quickly branched into healthcare, education, distribution, manufacturing, retail, construction, real estate, etc. His diversified portfolio generated many successes and some difficult cases.

In the mid-1990s, the family identified the need to enhance management resources to best manage a diversified asset base. A holding was formed as a regional asset management company. A Chairman and Vice Chairman were nominated and given a mandate. They were supposed to report to family members on a semi-annual basis. The vision conveyed a message of becoming a leading diversified asset management company investing in the GCC region with full adherence to Islamic practices and humanitarian principles. And the mission boiled down to generating superior risk-adjusted returns in its GCC investments by devising an asset allocation strategy through engaging and monitoring the best specialized managers for each discipline.

The organization was built around what we may term three SBUs:

• a Private Equity SBU with direct investments in unquoted private business based in UAE across various stages from Startup/Early stage to Expansion. Minimum ownership was to stand at 25 percent to 100 percent and minimum internal rate of return was to reach the 20 percent or more.

• a real estate SBU that invests in fully owned assets within the UAE.

• a public equity SBU that invests funds in publicly listed companies in the GCC stock exchanges with a minimum targeted return of 15 percent IRR.

What strikes the observer in the history of the company are two things. First is the shift from a conglomerate that is really concerned with managing businesses to a venture capital entity with interest in start ups and participation in existing ventures. The second is the marginalization of the core competency issue and the possible synergy that this would have created within the family firm.

Case 2: The making of a family CEO

CEOs of most family firms belong to family ranks or are very closely associated with them. Al Habtoor's CEO fulfills this condition but with a twist. His father, Khalaf Al Habtoor, founded the Al Habtoor Group in 1970 in recognition of Dubai's prospects. The following year the United Arab Emirates was formed, linking Dubai with its oil-rich neighbor Abu Dhabi at a time when Dubai ruler, Sheik Al Maktoum, was emerging as the visionary leader poised to transform Dubai into a global metropolis. Dubai thrived and the Al Habtoor Group took full advantage of that. A focus on construction in the early stages was followed by bold diversification into the conglomerate one sees today.

Financial data are invisible, but one does not have to go too far to put the revenues and assets at billions of US dollars. The father, Khalaf, remains chairman of the group, but CEO functions fell to the son: Mohammed (AME, 2004).

Mohammed Al Habtoor's degree from the United States in the late 1980s was of little use in his early days within his father's organization. At the time, the group owned its first hotel, the Metropolitan, and the son of the founder's expectations to walk straight into a management position, were quickly dispelled. He was asked to perform mundane jobs with the obvious goal of giving him firsthand experience at the minor details of the function. His later promotion to management ranks did not mean a smoother sailing as he was, according to his recollections, fired twice by his own father (AME, June 2004).

Today Mohammed Al Habtoor is chief executive officer of the Al Habtoor Group. The company portfolio includes an international network of hotels in Dubai, Lebanon, and Britain; eight major real estate developments currently underway; an engineering contractor; one of the largest schools in Dubai; and Bentley, Aston Martin, and Mitsubishi car dealerships.

It's a complex, highly diversified, rapidly growing organization, but Mohammud says the basic lessons of those early years are among the most critical to being successful. "I learned a great deal, particularly about consulting people. I may like to put gold windows on a building, but if four managers say silver is better, then silver it is. You have to listen to people".

We have seen what happens when the founder and chairman dies, he explains. "There can be disputes between the sons and the cousins, and the business is destroyed. It happens. For the continuity of the business it is best to go public, to have a board of directors, to be transparent."

Going public, however, is not an easy transition to make – especially for a family-run firm in the UAE. Al Habtoor Group has been seeking a listing in the UAE since 1998, but has yet to overcome all of the regulatory hurdles. Investors have been waiting for the shares in this conglomerate because of the performance and the comfortable finances. Funds raised by an eventual Al Habtoor IP could go towards financing the group's aggressive expansion strategy including its AED 1.8 billion (US$490 million) destined for a range of ambitious hospitality related construction projects in the UAE and Lebanon.

Observed strategic behavior

Exploiting opportunities created by the National Development Strategy of the States

Most of the family firms that we have been referring to achieved their prominence through a careful honing of opportunities made possible by the vision and economic development strategies of the rulers of the Emirates. Considerable government resources were put into that vision and those resources did boost the potential and the scope of those opportunities. Were it not for those opportunities family firms might have not found the fertile ground that they are exploring today.

Conglomeration

Investment made by most of the family businesses discussed above are of a conglomerate structure, i.e. unrelated in terms of markets, technologies, finance, or growth potential. Neither do they represent a core competency or a desire for that core competency. This is not a coincidence. It is an opportunistic response to the surge in demand and the craving for products and services.

Congruence with government strategies

A considerable volume of investments made by family firms are in response to massive government initiated projects especially in the real estate and hospitality sectors. The government took the lead and the family firms followed. This explains the heavy presence of family firms in construction, road building, hotels, residential blocks ...

Little R and D or innovation

Little of any investment made by a family firm in the GCC focuses on innovation or research and development. Most are straightforward trade, construction, hospitality, or simple manufacturing businesses. This, of course, is regrettable as it implies that technology transfer is limited, proprietor technology remains dominant, and a dependence on foreign sources of technology, little as that might be. It may also relate to the fact that many of these investments are in service industries where R and D is not central to the ultimate product and the desired function.

Little appetite for manufacturing

Family investments in the GCC have little connection with manufacturing or processing. As we said earlier, a considerable volume goes into trading, logistics, and, to a certain extent, financial services. The explanation could be the lengthy development process that manufacturing takes as well as the hefty investment it absorbs. Also the cumbersome cooperation agreements involved in transfer of technology and the maintenance and development of that technology.

Respect for scale

GCC family firms respect scale and decide, upon entry, to embark upon a scale-based investment. This is obvious in the size and scope of investment as diverse as real estate and retailing services. Whether it is the optimum scale or not, that is another matter. What matters is that they have an eye for large-scale coverage, large-scale production, and large- scale entry. The fact that some of those family firms are monopolies or quasi-monopolies may explain this disposition towards large-scale operations.

Absence of explicit SCA or Strategic Competitive Advantage (SCA)

The same abundant availability of capital and opportunities create an environment of disregard for core competency or the identification of an SCA. The result is heterogeneous portfolios and a wide scatter of businesses within one and the same entity. They are probably true "conglomerates" in the North American sense.

Summary and conclusions

Family-owned businesses feature heavily in almost every economy. There is ample evidence to that effect. Though generally fit for purpose, family firms may be weak. Their approach to management, strategy formulation, human resource mobilization, and succession may be questioned. Their visions are, occasionally, blurred. Their ability to carry the banner into the future is not always evident.

GCC family businesses are important in terms of size and contribution to the economy. They are predominantly large economic institutions with a key role in managing strategic sectors ranging from services to construction, trade and manufacturing. how family business could evolve into a massive nearly unmanageable scale.

These companies demonstrate a specific strategy formulation pattern that is typical for its opportunity orientation, scale demonstration, and government policy support.

8.2 When should an "Arab" entrepreneur call it quits?

The problem

Starting a new business is a process surrounded by an aura of excitement. The burning fire within the heart of the entrepreneur blends with new processes, people, faces, places, and events to produce an air of optimism. The nearest thing to it could be the feeling of waking up in the morning to find that your dream is, in fact, the reality. What this excitement conceals are two key questions that many entrepreneurs forget to ask themselves. The first is what am I in it for? What do I really want to achieve? The second question is what happens the day glamour is gone, the drive has become bumpy, and the tunnel has turned dark. Unfortunately these questions are either never asked or given casual consideration in the early stages of a new business, in many countries, and under different occasions as research reveals. They are, however, vital questions that should be seriously explored.

They are also especially vital in an Arab context. Two reasons account for that. First are culture and the strong impact of failure. Second is the prevalence of family business and the additional complication that this brings about.

Basic framework

What am I in it for?

Text books aside, motives for entry into business could cover a very wide array and reflect cultural norms and values that transcend conventional wisdom. The author's own cross- country observations can attest to that. Look, for example, at the group of female entrepreneurs in the Netherlands who cite collapsing marriages and imminent or actual divorce as the prime motive for their entry into business. Or the group of male entrepreneurs in Bei Hei (South East China) who state, in excited language, the desire to build something substantial for themselves and their families, a totally different perspective. And the dozen or so would-be entrepreneurs in Egypt who stressed the desire to fight against dim and unpromising job prospects in the country. These are anecdotes but they are illustrative of the very divergent motives that some entrepreneurs have for entry into business.

These intentions, goals, and reasons for being there are critical in the answer to the question what if? What if the venture fails and I am back to square one?

An entrepreneur should have from day one an explicit justification for entry into business and conditions that would render this reason null and void. He or she should have a clear mental image of what the personal goal is. Would that be:

- Growth through scale, merger, acquisition?
- Harvesting or sale of venture once a level of revenues, assets, or returns has been achieved?

- Continuity or seeking an element of revenue and asset stability at a given scale?
- "Melting-away" or integrating into larger businesses and disappearing as an independent business?
- Exit or termination of operations at the appearance of specific performance or personal signals?

What matters is that the alternatives are considered and one or more opted for before the start of operations. Minds may be changed if conditions change, but the basic assumption remains very much the prime consideration and the driving force behind strategic behavior.

The day strategies do not deliver results

Signs of trouble

When strategies do not work, the entrepreneur falls sick. Symptoms could vary but some could be performance-related and others could be person-related.

Performance-related signs of trouble

- Slow and declining cash flow. Cash flows at a certain pattern and pattern change is a sign of trouble. This is usually the earliest warning signal.
- Dry credit. Refusal of banks or other financial institutions either to grant credit or extend it to the venture is usually a sign of dire prospects.
- De-learning. Employees do not seem to learn from the tasks that they are performing. Their learning 'curve' is flat and their readiness to accept new challenges is limited.
- Unpaid family work. To tackle the problem of the increasing number of hours required to manage the increasing volume of problems, the entrepreneur spends more hours at work and asks family members to do the same. The problem is that those hours are not compensated for and they go unpaid.
- No repeat orders. Clients do not seem to come back. Repeat orders are not there. Customer loyalty has dissipated.
- Departure of key personnel. People the company relies on for key functions in operations, such as accounting, manufacturing, or distribution leave. Worse still they leave after long periods of association and a record of loyalty.
- Slow supplies. Suppliers are hesitant at taking the risk of providing supplies. They consider the entrepreneur an above-average risk that should be avoided.

Person-related signs of trouble

- Burnout. A degree of stress is inherent in each and every business. Going beyond the normal level is, however, a sign of burnout. This could be individual, collective, or even organizational.
- Unpaid hours. Unpaid family work has grave consequences for the home economics of the entrepreneur.
- Search for alternatives. Pressure of possible venture failure could drive the entrepreneur towards a search of paid employment as a safe haven.
- Marital frictions. Burnout conditions extol a price. One of the most common victims is the marriage of the entrepreneur.
- Mortgage of more personal assets. Financial pressure may lead to the entrepreneur's search for yet additional assets. First line collateral may not be enough and second line assets may provide the only target.

And all these symptoms lead to one of three states of sickness:

1. **Permanently recoverable.** That is a situation when the basic tenets or the core competences of the business are solid and preserved but performance of the business function is bad.
2. **Nearly recoverable.** This is a state where the core competences are being challenged but intervention could re-establish viability. It could also be a situation where the core-competences are not developed yet and they have to develop to sustain existence.
3. **Non-recoverable or "End game".** This is when the core competences and the environmental conditions are hostile and there is little likelihood that normal conduct of the business can continue. This could happen if demand for the industry's product collapses (competition, substitutes, cost, regulation, etc); the technology is not sustainable (costly, hazardous, too complex, etc), finance stream is cut permanently, etc.

The day I should call it quits

This decision is dependent on the seriousness of the problems and the urgency of the situation. The entrepreneur, or an external agency, should try to diagnose the state of the venture and develop a realistic picture of the situation. Is it a recoverable, nearly recoverable or 'end game' situation? Figure 8.2 is an attempt at that. What it provides is a listing of key problems and an opportunity to grade them as either serious, of average proportion, or not serious (manageable, urgent, and critical). Also an opportunity to weigh each of those factors according to the seriousness of the issue. This seriousness is both objective and subjective depending on the company's situation and the individual circumstances of the entrepreneur. There is also the point of balance between business-related performance problems and individual problems. That point of balance is the sole prerogative of the entrepreneur. A weighted average score should emerge for the business-related factors as well as the individual-related factors. These could be one of four combinations:

1. High business performance related score combined with a high individual-related score. A serious situation reflecting problems at all fronts
2. High business performance-related score combined with a low individual-related score. An unusual situation that embodies a business failure combined with individual "satisfaction."
3. Low business performance-related score combined with a low individual-related score. A workable situation.
4. Low business performance-related score combined with a high individual-related score. A serious situation reflecting problems with the entrepreneur.

A combination of these weighted average scores should lead to the basic decision to opt for one or more of a set of strategic options (see Figure 8.2):

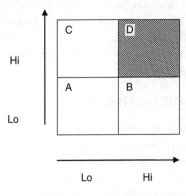

Figure 8.2   Four different strategic responses

- Segment A. Accommodation or seek conventional solutions to both problems as the level does not warrant a dramatic intervention.
- Segment B. Baseline examination or grass root problem is at hand. The entrepreneur's own ability to manage is challenged. Exit may be the answer.
- Segment C. Critical turnaround is needed or a restructuring of operations.
- Segment D. Death is imminent. Terminate venture as the problem levels are too high for an attempt at repair. It is very likely that the business-related problems have undermined the core competences of the venture.

The following figure (Figure 8.3) provides an operational instrument for the grading of business performance related problems.

Problem area	Specific problem	State of the problem			Weight given to the specific factor
		Manageable	Urgent	Critical	
Business performance-related	Insolvency coefficient (see annex)				
	Declining cash flow				
	Dry credit				
	Unpaid work				
	De learning				
	Departure of key personnel				
	Late supplies				
Weighted average Score (weights are estimated by the entrepreneur)					
Person-related	Burnout				
	Unpaid work				
	Mortgage of personal assets				
	Marriage-related frictions				
Weighted average Score					

Figure 8.3   The grading of business performance-related problems

Is there life after death? Can I re-enter?

Re-entry thoughts usually occur in the minds of those who:

- Attribute venture failure to extreme environmental conditions that they could not influence.
- See opportunities in different industries altogether.
- Are encouraged by their immediate associates (family, friends) to give it "another try".
- Value the learning impact of the first venture and wish to put that to use in another one.

The decision is by no means easy especially for those who's first, or second, venture failure had far reaching implications. It is the desire to achieve, the urge to fulfill dreams, the longing for recognition that drives those towards a new entry. Culture plays a serious role here. There can be a sense of shame induced by business failure in certain culture that is difficult to circumvent. It is actually a blend of shame, agony, rejection on top of non-achievement.

The situation of the Arab entrepreneur

The analysis that we have gone through so far should apply to Arab entrepreneurs as much as to any other entrepreneur elsewhere. Culture may restrain this applicability, however.

Cultural traits and forces may render the exit decision of an Arab entrepreneur a difficult proposition. Hofstede's analysis of culture's dimensions and its consequences (Hofstede, 1984) could extend a helping hand here. Let us recall that Arab countries reveal a situation where power distance and uncertainty avoidance are high (an index of 80 and 68 respectively compared to a world average ranking of 51 and 64) and individualism is low (38 compared to a world average ranking of 68). This implies an inequality in the distribution of power and wealth and a low level of tolerance for uncertainty and ambiguity within society. It equally implies a basic mistrust of ways and means of gaining power and distribution of wealth. And the low individualism index translates into a close long-term commitment and absolute loyalty to the member "group", whether family, extended family, or extended relationships.

Table 8.1 Culture's dimensions index according to Hofstede

Culture's dimension	Arab countries index	Average world index
Power distance	80	51
Uncertainty avoidance	68	64
Individualism	38	68
Masculinity	53	51

Source: Hofstede, 1984

Three of those cultural attributes could have an impact on the exit decision by the entrepreneur.

• Power distance. High power distance index is very likely to encourage limited feed back and late realization of the existence of exit triggers.

• Uncertainty avoidance. High uncertainty avoidance is very likely to limit the ability to deal with the gray outlook and the unpromising outlook.

• Individualism. Low individualism may encourage search for a collective solution but that could only work if issues of face are not an obstacle. Face is a strong factor in communications in Arab countries, though. And family firms work with a measure of collective decision making.

Let me reiterate that data on genuine exit strategies are scarce in Arab countries (and non-Arab countries too). The associated sense of failure and loss of face makes exploration or analysis of the issue, within an Arab context, rather difficult.

Summary and conclusions

The issue of death of a venture and the decision to terminate operations are intricate and difficult to explore. The chapter provides a conceptual and operational framework and then tries to apply that to the Arab situation. The conceptual and operational framework assumes first that the entrepreneur knows why the venture is being embarked on and with what vision of the future. Failure seldom comes to mind at this stage. If failure occurs, it is either the result of personal malfunctioning or business mal-performance.

And the solution is a careful weighing of the significance of each factor and the development of a final view of the feasibility of continuity.

Arab entrepreneurs would face three hurdles when trying to take this decision and all of them are culture related. First is the high power distance, second is individualism, and the third is uncertainty avoidance.

Annex

Predicting bankruptcy

Source: www.bnkruptcyaction.com/bankpred2.htm

The above mentioned link provides the software that handles the calculation. The authors claim that this Bankruptcy Predictor has proved to have an accuracy rate of over 88 percent for small businesses (average asset size US$2.5 million) and an accuracy rate of over 83 percent for very large businesses (average asset size US$63.4 million). A negative score predicts bankruptcy.

Variable	Performance level	Variable	Performance level
Current Assets		Sales	
Interest Expense		Total Assets	
Profit or loss before taxes		Current liabilities	

Calculate score

The higher the score, the more financially sound is the company. The lower the score, the greater the danger of the company becoming insolvent. This technique should be considered complementary to other tools. The formula used is the "Springate Formula" developed at Simon Fraser University, Burnaby, British Columbia.

Bibliography

ABIC, Annual Report 2005.

Airline Business, November 16, 2006.

Albert, M. (1993), *Capitalism vs. Capitalism*. London: Whurr Publishers.

Al-Ghamdi, S., Sohail and M. Sadiq (2006), Sustaining competitive advantage in the global petrochemical industry: a Saudi Arabian perspective, *Journal for International Business and Entrepreneurship Development* 3(1/2), 2006.

Al-Sa'doun, A. (2006), Five Strategies Drive Saudi Arabia's Petchem Industry Growth, February 2006 RED ORBT.

Andrews, K. (1971), *The Concept of Corporate Strategy*, Dow Jones-Irwin, Homewood, Illinois.

Ansoff, I. (1965), *Corporate Strategy*, McGraw-Hill, New York.

Ansoff, I. (1969), *Business Strategy*, Penguin Books, Harmondsworth.

Ansoff, I. (1976), *From Strategic Planning to Strategic Management*, Wiley, London.

Anthony, R. and Govindarajan, V. (2001), *Management Control Systems* (10th ed.), McGraw Hill/Irwin, Boston.

Arab News, People Have Underestimated the Strength of SABIC, Monday, October 2, 2006.

Argentini, J. (1976), *Corporate Collapse*, New York McGraw Hill.

Babson College, London Business School (2005).

Boulding, K. (1956), General systems theory, the skeleton of science, *Management Science*, April 2.

Buckman, R. Venture capital floods 'Chinese garages', *The Wall Street Journal*, July 28, 2005.

Business Week, August 11, 2003.

Business Week, Harvard Guru to Help Libya, Europe, February 20, 2007.

Bygrave, W. and Hunt, S. (2005), Global Entrepreneurship Monitor and Gem Financing Report 2004, Babson College.

Canadian Ministry of Industry (1997), Bankruptcy in Canada.

Challenges ahead, interview with Minister G Al Rifai, Minister of Economy and Foreign Trade, Emerging Syria, Oxford Business Group (2002).

Charles, W., Hill, L. and Gareth R. Jones (2004), *Strategic Management*, Houghton Mifflin.

Chester A. C. (1998), Are we Americans still capable of thinking strategically? USIP.

Cox, L.W. and Camp, S.M. (2001), International Survey of Entrepreneurs: 2001, Executive Report.

Crocker, C. (1998), Are we Americans stillcapable of thinking strategically? USIP, News Release, August 20.

Drucker, P. Entrepreneurship in Business Enterprise, *Journal of Business Policy*, 1, 1970.

Drucker, P. (2001), The Essentials of Drucker: Selections from the management works of Peter F. Drucker. New York: Harper Business.

Easy Oz – Emirates Airline, Low cost is coming to long haul flights, next could be low fares, *The Economist*, October 29, 2005.

Egypt vulnerable in post-2005 clothing scenario, Egytex International Apparel and Home Textile Manufacturing Trade Fair 2004, Hong Kong Trade Development Council, *International Market News*, May 20, 2004.

El Namaki, M. (1988), Encouraging entrepreneurs in developing countries, *Long Range Planning* Vol.4.

El Namaki, M. (1989), Management training for small and medium industries: a cross country analysis of characteristics, constraints and catalysts, in *Proceedings of the Second Tokyo Conference on Management Development of Small and Medium Sized Enterprises in Asia*, Tokyo, Foundation for Asian management Development.

El Namaki, M. (1989), The strategic positioning of the newly industrialized countries (NICs) in the international market, in (R. Lamb, Ed) *Advances in Strategic Management*, Voloume 4.

El Namaki, M. (1990), Small business – The myths and the reality, *Long Range Planning*, 23(4) pp. 78–87.

El Namaki, M. (1992), Creating corporate vision, *Long Range Planning*, Vol. 25, No. 6.

El Namaki, M. (1996), *The Contemporary Dynamics of Entrepreneurship*, Journal of International business and entrepreneurship (JIBE) Vol.5, No. 2.

El Namaki, M. (1999), *A Conceptual Framework for Economic and Corporate Restructuring, Strategic issues at the dawn of a new millennium*, Lansa Publishing.

El Namaki, M. Have You Lost Control? *Capital Magazine*, April, 2006.

Emirates Airline – A product of vision, *New Nation* Online Edition, Sat., May 20, 2006.

Emirates Airlines to offer in-flight iPod connection in '07, *The Wall Street Journal*, November 14, 2006.

Emirates boss heads for bigger goals, *The Sunday Times*, Times Newspapers Ltd., London, July 23, 2006.

Emirates Group Annual Report 2005–2006.

EOS Gallup Europe (2004), Flash EB No 146, Entrepreneurship.

EU Flasheuroparameter, Entrepreneurship, January 2004.

Family business statistics, Boston Globe, May 4, 2003.

Family-run firms are urged to adapt to global changes, *Khaleej Times*, February 12, 2006.

Financial Times (Farnborough Air Show–Boeing lands $ 3.3bn Emirates order), UK Edition, London, July 19, 2006.

Flanagan, the elder statesman of Emirates, *Airline Business*, November 16, 2005.

Flights of fancy, *The Economist*, October 5, 2006.

Gerschenkron, A. (1962), *Economic Backwardness in Historical Perspective*, Cambridge: Harvard University Press.

Gibb, A.A. (1999), 'Creating an Entrepreneurial Culture in Support of SMEs' small Enterprise Development. *An International Journal*. Vol.10. No. 4.

GEM, Global Entrepreneurship Monitor (2002), 2002 Summary Report, 30 November 2002, Babson College, Ewing Marion Kauffman Foundation, London Business School.

Global Entrepreneurship Monitor and Gem Financing Report 2004.

GEM, Global Entrepreneurship Monitor (2005), 2004 Financing Report, Babson College, London Business School.

Goldsmith, A. (1995), Making managers more effective: Applications of strategic management, *Working Papers*, USAID's Implementing Policy Change Project, Working Paper No. 9, March 1995.

Goodman, J. B. and Loveman G. W. (1991), Does privatization serve the public interest?, *Harvard Business Review*, Boston, November/December 1991. pp. 26–38.

Gygrave, W., Reynolds P., Autio, E. and Hay, M. (2002), Global entrepreneurship monitor 2002 summary report, Babson College.

Kurt Christensen, H. K. (1988), Diagnosis for General Managers, Kellogg Graduate School of Management.

Hamel, G. and Prahalad, C. K. (1989), Strategic Intent, *Harvard Business Review*, (May-June): p. 63–76.

Hamel, G and Prahalad, C. K. (1990), The Core Competence of the Corporation, *Harvard Business Review*, May-June, 79–91.

Hamel, G. and Prahalad, C. K. (1994), *Competing for the Future: Breakthrough Strategies for Seizing Control of Your Industry and Creating the Markets of Tomorrow.* Boston: Harvard Business School Press.

Handy, C. B. (1985), *Understanding Organizations (3rd Ed)*, Harmondsworth: Penguin Books.

Harvard Guru to Help Libya, *Business Week Europe* February 20, 2007.

Hill, C. and Jones, G. (2004), *Strategic Management: An Integrated Approach.* (6th edition) Boston: Houghton Mifflin.

Hofstede, G. (1984), *Culture's consequences*, Sage Publications, Newbury Park, California.

ILO, Laborstat, 2004, (Internet)/International Labour Statistics.

International Energy Agency, Key World Energy Statistics (2006).

International Energy Outlook, Energy Information Administration, US government, June 2006.

International Labour Office database on labor statistics (2005), ILO Bureau of Statistics.

Interview with Minister of the Public Enterprise Sector. *Al Ahram Weekly*, Issue No. 574 on line, February 21–27, 2002.

Jayid, A. Ahmed (1995), Privatization in Arab Countries, Paper presented before a conference on Development Economics, the Norwegian School in Economics and Business Administration, Bergen Norway.

Jonsson Yinya Li, Investing in China: the Emerging Venture Capital Industry in China, *Asia Times*, September 3, 2005.

Kaplan, R. S. and Norton, D. P. (1992), The Balanced Scorecard – Measures That Drive Performance, *Harvard Business Review* (January–February).

Kaplan, R. and Norton, D. (1996), Using the balanced scorecard as a strategic management system. *Harvard Business Review* (January–February).

Kets de Vries, M. (1985), The Dark Side of Entrepreneurship, *Harvard Business Review*.

Kim-Song Tan and Sock-Yong Phang (2005) From efficiency-driven to innovation-driven economic growth, Perspectives from Singapore, Vol. 1 of 1. The World Bank.

Knowledge @ Wharton (2004). In Asia, the Venture Capital Business Has Two Sides, January 22.

Liedkta, J., Linking strategic thinking with strategic planning, *Strategy and Leadership*, September–October 26, 1998.

McClelland, D. (1961), *The Achieving Society*, Van Nostrand, Princeton NJ.

McCombs, B. (1991), *Metacognition and Motivation in Higher Level Thinking*, Paper presented at the annual meeting of the American Educational Research Association Chicago, IL.

Mintzberg, H. (1973), *The Nature of Managerial Work*, New York, Harper & Row.

Mintzberg, H. (1992), *Five Ps for Strategy in The Strategy Process*, H. Mintzberg and JB. Quinn eds., Prentice-Hall International Editions, Englewood Cliffs NJ.

Mintzberg, H. (1994), *The Rise and fall of Strategic Planning*, Free Press, (New York and Toronto).

Mohamed H. Al-Mady, SABIC Vice Chairman and CEO, Putting the Middle East at the Center of the Petrochemical Industry: Strategies for Long-term Success 2007.

Patrick, T. (2004), Boss accused over Polaroid failure, *Mail on Sunday*, April 18, 2004.

Pettijohn, T. F. (1999), Psychology: A ConnecText, 4th edition, McGraw Hill.

Pinchot, G. (1985), *Intrapreneuring: Why You Don't Have to Become an Entrepreneur.* New York, Harper and Row.

Political spin off effects, *Al Ahram Weekly*, 30 June–6 July 2005.

Pondering Partnership, interview with consultant Aiman Abd El Nour, Emerging Syria, Oxford Business Group (2002).

Porter, M. (2001) The competitive advantage of Singapore transition to innovation stage, New Economy Conference, Singapore.

Porter, M. E. (1990), Competitive Advantage of Nations, The Free Press.

Porter, M. E (1980), *Competitive Strategy: Techniques for Analyzing Industries and Competitors*, New York, Free Press.

Porter, M. E. (1996), What is Strategy? *Harvard Business Review*, November-December.

Porter, M. E. (1998), *The Competitive Advantage of Nations*, New York, Free Press.

Privatization amended. *Al Ahram Weekly*, June 8–14, 2006.

Privatization phase out? *Al-Ahram Weekly*. Online, February 14–20, 2002.

Profile: The making of Mohammed Al Habtoor, AME Info, June 2, 2004.

Ram, C. and Useem, J. (2002), Why Companies Fail, *Fortune Magazine* May 27, 2002.

Random House Unabridged Dictionary, © Random House, Inc. 2006.

Ray, J. J. A Quick Measure of Achievement Motivation – Validated in Australia and Reliable in Britain and South Africa, *Australian Psychologist*, 14(3), 1979, pp. 337–344.

Red Orbit (2006), Five Strategies Drive Saudi Arabia's Petrochemical Industry Growth, February 9, 2006.

Rigas Doganis (2001), *The Airline Business in the 21st Century*, New York, Routledge.

Row erupts between Qantas and Emirates, *The Financial Times*, UK Edition, November 9, 2005.

SABIC Annual Report, 2005.

Safan, S. (2000), *Essays in Economics and Management in Syria*, Arabic language edition. 21 Century Publications, Damascus (Syria).

Safan, S. (2002), *Going to Market*, the Oxford Business Group.

Sajjad M. Jasimuddin (2001), Analyzing the competitive advantages of Saudi Arabia with Porter's model, *The Journal of Business & Industrial Marketing*. Santa Barbara, 16(1).

Samuel, B. and Edwards, R. (1993), *Understanding Capitalism*. Harper Collins.

Samuelson P., Nordhaus, D. and Mandel, J. (1995), *Economics*, New York, McGraw Hill.

Schumpeter, J. (1942), *Capitalism, Socialism and Democracy*. New York: Harper and Row.

Schumpeter, J. (1950), *Capitalism, Socialism and Democracy*, 3rd edition, New York, Harper and Row.

Schumpeter, J. (1984), *Capitalism, Socialism and Democracy*, Harper Torchbooks.

Shirley, M. (1998), The Experience with Privatization, *Finance & Development*. The World Bank & IMF. 25(3), 1998, pp. 34–35.

Small Firms. Findings from the 1998 Survey of Small Business Finance.

Sobel, R. (1974), *The Entrepreneurs: Explorations within the American Business Tradition.* New York, Weybright and Talley.

Sound Corporate Governance Essential to Family Businesses Success, *Zawya* January 25, 2007.

Spreng, D. (2005), It's Time for Venture Capital Firms to Grow Up, *Venture Capital Journal*.

Strategic Capital Management AG (2005), Global Private Equity performance review (2004).

Strategic issues at the dawn of a new millennium, Lansa Publishing.

Stephen, J., Dorgan, J., Dowdy, J. and Thomas M. Rippin. (2007) Who should – and shouldn't – run the family business, *The McKinsey Quarterly*, October 6.

Successful business needs more than family, *Gulf News*, April 1, 2007.

The Economist, Credit where credit is due, March 18, 1999.

The Economist, Flights of fancy, www.economist.com, October 5, 2006.

The American Heritage® Dictionary of the English Language, 4th edition. Houghton Mifflin Company, 2006.

The McKinsey Quarterly, October 6, 2007.

The only way is up, macroeconomic analysis, *Emerging Syria*, Oxford Business Group (2000).

The Syria Report (2002), Restructuring is going on in public organizations.

Thierry, V., Noelle, D., Mazzarol, T. and Thein, V. Triggers and Barriers Affecting Entrepreneurial Intentionality.

Thompson, Arthur A., Jr. Strickland III, A. J. and Kramer, T. R. (1998). Readings in Strategic Management. 10th edition, Boston, Irwin/McGraw Hill.

Treading a fine line, Emerging Syria, Oxford Business Group (2002).

United States Small Business Administration (2003), Financing Patterns of the small business economy 2003–2004, US Small Business Administration, 2005.

United States Small Business Administration (2005), Small business and micro business lending in the United States for data years 2002–2003, Office of Advocacy, United States Small Business Administration, Washington, March 2005.

USAID, the impact of privatization and policy reform on cotton spinning industry in Egypt, Report No 15, November 2000.

White, S., GAO, J. and Zhang, W. (2002), China's venture capital industry: institutional trajectories and system structure, paper submitted to the international *Conference on Financial Systems, Corporate Investment in Innovation and Venture Capital*, Brussels 7 and 8 November 2002.

Wilken, P. (1979), *Entrepreneurship: A Comparative and Historical Study*, Norwood, N J Ablex.

World Bank (2004a), Syria Fact Sheet, World Bank.

World Bank (2004b), World Development Indicators.

World Bank Country Fact Sheets, World Bank, 2004–2005.

World Economic Forum (2003), The Global Competitiveness Report, 2002–2003.

World Economic Forum (2004), The Global Competitiveness Report, 2003–2004.

World Economic Forum (2005), Global Competitiveness Report, 2004–2005.

World Economic Forum (2006), interview with Mohamed Al-Mady, CEO, SABIC.

World Economic Forum, Global Competitiveness Report, 2006.

World Economic Forum, Interview with Mohamed Al-Mady, CEO, SABIC, 2006.

World wide look at reserves and production, *Oil and Gas Journal*, 103 (47), 2005.

Zero2ipo Venture Capital Research Center (2005), China venture capital semi annual report.

Index